Chambers
Adult Learners'
Guide to Spelling

Chambers
Adult Learners'
Guide to Spelling

Anne Betteridge

Chambers

CHAMBERS

An imprint of Chambers Harrap Publishers Ltd
7 Hopetoun Crescent
Edinburgh, EH7 4AY

First published by Chambers Harrap Publishers Ltd 2008

A CIP catalogue record for this book is available from the British Library.

ISBN 978 0550 10355 0

Extract on page 109 based on a longer poem by Jerrold H. Zar, originally published in
the Journal of Irreproducible Results, January/February 1994.

Dyslexia screening checklist on pages 144–5 reproduced by permission of LLU+,
London South Bank University.

Editor: Mary O'Neill
Prepress: Nicolas Echallier, Becky Pickard
Illustrations: on pages 5, 9, 11, 19, 39, 42, 45, 46, 72, 75, 99, 102: Mike Flanagan;
on pages 87, 88, 92: Lee Fullarton; on pages 70, 71, 73, 74, 76, 124: Andrew Laycock

Designed by Chambers Harrap Publishers Ltd, Edinburgh
Typeset by Gill McColl
Printed in Italy, by LEGO SpA, Lavis TN

Contents

Introduction

About this book

Chambers Adult Learners' Guide to Spelling is for you if you find spelling difficult. It is about breaking up words and learning how to remember them in a different way. It is not about the dreaded spelling rules!

Follow the routine described in the book and you will learn to spell at least twenty words in the next four weeks but, just as importantly, you will discover how to learn many more.

You **can** improve your spelling. You will then have more confidence in your writing skills and, for example, feel much better about filling in forms, writing letters and using the computer. Although computers usually have a spellchecker, this won't distinguish between all the words which sound the same but are spelt differently.

Many of you will have struggled for years to improve your spelling and it won't surprise you to know that there isn't a magic wand to wave over your difficulties. You might have been taught to just keep copying, over and over again, the word you want to learn. For some people that will work, for reasons that you will discover later on. For other people it might work in the short term but it won't last. The routine I will describe will ensure that the spelling will stay with you forever.

The instructions are deliberately kept simple. This is a book free from technical terms and jargon that only language specialists would understand. Occasionally, a rule is mentioned but I have only included those that are straightforward and that might help you. In most cases it is better to tackle the word that you want to learn without thinking about any of the rules that might apply.

How to use this book

The book is in four sections:

1. Part A covers some of the basic things you will need to know before you get started.

2. Part B shows you how to break words into smaller chunks.

3. Part C (on the pages with a blue frame) explains clearly how to learn your own spellings over a four-week period. After the four weeks you will be able to spell words that you cannot spell now.

4. Part D gives you some useful information on subjects connected with spelling.

Make sure you read at least the first two parts before starting to learn your own words. All the help you need will be found here and you can re-read it as often as you want.

You will learn words that you have chosen, not ones that I think might be useful. You might often want to write a note to school, or pass on a phone message at work, but always lack confidence in your ability to spell each word correctly. You will find it more useful to learn words that you use regularly, rather than words that you don't use very often.

As well as this book, you will need a small notebook and some highlighter pens. It will be helpful if you can find a quiet and comfortable place when you want to study on your own. Try to make sure that you won't be disturbed.

Real People

Many of the examples in the book have come from students I have worked with and they are words that they learned to spell using the methods you will follow. I have worked with people aged between 16 and 82. They all struggled with spelling, both at school and as adults. Each of them now feels much better about it and they all continue to use the same methods, now that they are learning spellings on their own.

Acknowledgements

I very much appreciate the part that LLU+ has played in the development of my awareness of spelling-related issues. LLU+ is part of London South Bank University. Their commitment to recognize and respond to the difficulties that some adults have with spelling has prompted me to take that theme in a slightly different direction by putting together this self-access book. In particular, I would like to thank Ross Cooper and Alexandra Davies.

Thanks to Margaret Dawson and Miriam Sampson for being my role models and confidence boosters.

Thank you also to Jem, Jenna and Colin for all your encouragement and support.

About the author

Anne Betteridge is an dyslexia assessor and tutor, and an adult literacy specialist. She has taught for many years in Further Education colleges, and worked for national organizations including Dyslexia Action (formerly The Dyslexia Institute) and the Basic Skills Agency.

PART A

THE BASICS OF SPELLING

Basic principles

The following principles are guidelines for you to refer back to as often as you want. You won't have to learn them parrot fashion but it will be helpful if you read them through now, then come back and read them again when you are about to start learning your words.

1.   Break the words into small chunks.

Most of us feel confident about spelling short words. It is the longer words that are the problem. Separating a long word into smaller bits is like working with short words. This makes long words much easier to learn. You will be shown six ways of breaking up words and you will see very quickly how many of our longer words are just two or more chunks stuck together. When you split up a word aim for groups of roughly three letters and try not to leave one letter on its own.

Even if you find short words difficult there will be a method to help you.

2.   Use more than one sense.

The greater the number of your senses you use, the more likely you are to remember the word because each different sense will give you a better chance of anchoring it in your memory. Seeing and hearing are the senses we use most often when spelling but we can also use touch and movement. For instance, rather than just looking at a word, say it out loud and try to hear the separate sounds in it. If you have some magnetic letters on your fridge then use them to make the word.

Our motor memory can be very strong – the feel or movement of an action can be recorded in the same way as a sound or a picture. You will see how this can be important for spelling when you come to the topic of handwriting.

- Visual memory – what we remember by using our eyes
- Auditory memory – what we remember by using our ears
- Motor memory – what we remember by using movement

3. Use different levels of memory.

Sometimes your memory will cope with a word very easily once you see it in smaller sections. For other words you will have to make your memory work harder. Be prepared to include extra information when necessary. You will see a diagram later in this part of the book showing the different ways of digging deep into your memory to ensure that you will remember a word forever.

4. Practise regularly.

It will be very important to practise your spellings each day for a week. The good news is that each practice will only take one or two minutes! I have found that people who commit themselves to a daily practice are the ones who become the better spellers. Those who try to get away with just looking at their words two or three times a week are, unfortunately, not able to remember those words forever.

You may think that you know the word after the second or third day. Even if this happens you should still continue with the suggested method for the rest of the week. It is important to remember that you are not testing yourself each day, you're just practising the strategy for each word. Your regular practices will pay off in the end.

(You may have noticed the two different spellings of **practise** and **practice** in the paragraphs above. They are both correct! If you can learn the difference between these two words, and how to use them, you will be better than many so-called 'good' spellers. I'll show you how to do this when you reach the section on *Word families*.)

As you go through the book you will see the following symbols:

If you see a word with a star * it means that it is an incorrect spelling:

   *rong

Word sounds will be shown like this:

   /sh/

Names of letters will be written:

   'a'   'b'   'c'

Memory

Your memory is a strange thing. You are more likely to remember something that is a bit odd, than something that is normal. If it is funny or rude, then so much the better! If a clown walked past you in the street you would remember him the next day, or the next week, but you probably wouldn't remember all the people who were dressed normally. So, if you imagine a

bra in a li**bra**ry

you will remember how to spell that tricky word.

We are also very good at learning something new if we link it with something we already know. If you can cook a meal for one person, then you can probably cook a special meal for six by using the knowledge you used when cooking for one.

If you know how to spell

H**igh** Street   because you live there,

then linking it with a word you don't know, such as

e**igh**t

will help you to remember how to spell 'e**igh**t', the new word.

(Perhaps **e.t.** lives at 8 H**igh** Street?)

We are good at remembering diagrams, pictures, shapes and colour but we are **not** so good when it comes to small, black marks on white paper. So, trying to remember which letters are in which word, and in which order, will be very difficult for some people.

We can use pictures, shapes and colour whenever the word gets particularly difficult.

The word 'daily' makes a shape which is not the same as most other words:

You may find that the shape of the word, with some colour added, is easier to remember than just the letters on their own. For some people it will make very little difference but for others, seeing the shape can have a huge impact.

Making a picture out of a difficult word will give your brain a better chance of remembering it.

Some people find it helpful to make a bus out of the first three letters of 'business':

bus iness

You could imagine a group of people on a yacht to help you remember the word 'they'. Use a word you already know – 'the' – and add the letter 'y' which is the first letter of yacht:

Just highlighting different parts of a word may be all that is needed.

Our memories need the information over and over again before we can be sure that it will stay forever. Even then, if we don't use it every so often, it will go. Most of us are not able to see something once and remember it. We need to see it several times. This is why, when following the routine, you'll look at the same information each day for seven days. By the end of the week you should find that the new information you have given your memory will stay there, especially if you use it again soon.

Breaking up words

Some people are good at remembering the **sounds** in a word. Others are better at knowing what a word **looks** like. Once you have read through Part B you should get a feel for which you prefer. Some of the strategies rely on you being able to hear different parts of words; the others rely on you being able to recognize, or visualize, sections of a word. Knowing your own particular strengths will be helpful because it makes more sense to work with your strengths rather than your weaknesses.

However, it will be important to try all the methods of breaking up words during the four weeks. It is better to use as many different ways as you can to start with because not all the words you want to learn will work by just using one method. By doing that, you will eventually be able to work out your own strengths. Later on you may find that you prefer to use one or two methods most of the time.

Reading and writing

Regular reading will improve your spelling because you are looking at words and, hopefully, storing them away in your visual memory. Your visual memory is like a filing cabinet full of the pictures, or shapes, of words. Good readers read by just looking very quickly at a word and recognizing its shape.

Even more useful will be doing more of what weak spellers don't like – writing! When you **read**, the correct spellings are on the page in front of you. When you **write**, you have to find the spellings from your memory's filing system, which may be in a bit of a muddle. The more often you task your brain with finding the words you want, the more the word will stick. Brains are naturally quite lazy but you can improve your filing system if you make your brain work harder.

Using memory levels

A good speller is good at remembering all the letters in a word and in which order the letters appear. They often have good visual memories which means that they have stored away an accurate picture of the word. Some people are very lucky and seem to just remember the words from when they learned them at school. Others don't have that natural memory and have to work hard at remembering the spellings they need.

We all have different depths of memory that we can tap into. If we use the first level it means that we don't need to give the brain much information to help us remember something. The deeper we go, the more information we need to supply. Using the very deepest layer means that we need to provide lots of extra information in order to help the brain remember.

Every time we add in another sense then we are adding another layer of memory.

Everyone is different. Some people will need only one or two layers of memory in order to remember how to spell a word. Others will need three, four or even five. You may always have to go to level four or five if you find it very difficult to remember the letters in a word. Some people find spelling so difficult that they need a picture to help with every part of their address, for instance.

The word 'separate' is not easy to spell. Many people get it wrong. It often appears as *seperate on signs, in brochures and on websites. Look at the different levels of memory that you could use if you want to remember this word:

Separate

FIRST LEVEL

Just notice the hard part.

See and think

It's an 'a' not an 'e'.

SECOND LEVEL

Find something to remember.

See, say and hear

"There is a **rat** in it."

THIRD LEVEL

Link with the meaning of the word.

See, say, hear and imagine

"It is important to sep**arat**e **a rat** from a mouse."

FOURTH LEVEL

Draw a picture which links the meaning with the actual word.

See, say, hear, draw and move

"It is important to sep**arat**e **a rat** from a mouse."

It is important to sep**arat**e **a rat** from a mouse.

FIFTH LEVEL

Use plastic letters to make the word. Move the small words out of the bigger word to see them on their own.

See, say, hear, draw, touch and move

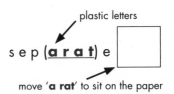

plastic letters

s e p (**a r a t**) e

move '**a rat**' to sit on the paper

This method of breaking up the word is described in the section *Small words*.

Your drawings **do not** need to be works of art – you just need to easily understand and remember them!

SID

Meet Sid.

He takes life very slowly. His name comes from the words

Slow

It

Down

For most people who find spelling hard, 'slowing it down' will make a big difference. By giving your brain the chance to take in each bit of a word slowly, it will stop the whole thing feeling jumbled up. Slowing it down will trick the brain into thinking that it is dealing with two or three small words, rather than one long word.

You will find that, no matter how you have broken up the word, tackling it slowly will give you a better chance of learning it.

When you see SID in the pages to come, remember to

Slow ... It ... Down ...

PART B

BREAKING UP WORDS

This part of the book shows you the six ways of breaking up words:

- *Small words*
- *Prefixes and suffixes*
- *Say it oddly*
- *Syllables*
- *Memory tricks*
- *Word families*

Each strategy will be explained in the following pages with examples of words which can be learned using each method. Of course, there isn't only one way to learn a word – you might think of a different method which will be more memorable for you. The examples are just to give you an idea of how to use that particular method. The most memorable strategies for learning spellings are the ones that you come up with yourself. One student learned to spell 'electric**ian**' because her brother was called **Ian**. He was good at electrical jobs so she was able to visualize him as an electrician!

Some of the methods will overlap and you will find that you can use more than one method with some words. For instance, you can see that 'Saturday' contains two helpful *Small words* (shown in blue):

Sat ur **day**

but it also breaks into *Syllables*

Sat/ur/day

in the same way.

In the word 'dangerous' you can pick out either of two *Small words* (shown in blue):

danger ous

d **anger** ous

but it also has a *Suffix*

danger(ous)

Breaking up words

Sometimes a word can be broken up in several ways:

Small word	h **ear** ing
Suffix	hear(ing)
Syllables	hear/ing
Word families	n**ear**, r**ear**, d**ear**, f**ear**
Say it oddly	he / a / ring
Memory trick	You h**ear** with your **ear**.

You can then choose the one you are most likely to remember.

You will be given enough information to help you to look at words in a different way and to be able to break them up. Once you understand the six methods you will be able to work out which will be most helpful for the words you want to learn.

Small words

As soon as you break up a word it becomes easier to manage, and finding something inside it which you recognize can be a great relief. Many words have shorter words inside them. The English language is a difficult language when it comes to spelling but one good thing about it is that it contains patterns of letters which are repeated again and again. This is why we can find so many words inside other words.

Looking for smaller words is particularly useful when the pronunciation of the word 'hides' some of the letters. It is perfectly natural to say the word 'vegetable' as though we were saying 'veg' followed by 'table'. The pronunciation doesn't allow us hear that there is another 'e' in the middle of the word. So, if you focus on the small word 'get' in the middle of 've**get**able', when you come to spell the word you will **get** it right.

People often think that their spelling problems stem from the way they speak. This can be the case sometimes, particularly when the /th/ sound is pronounced /f/. This results, for example, in the word 'three' becoming 'free' and can cause confusion with the meaning as well as the spelling. Most of the time, however, it is not the way someone says a word that causes the spelling difficulties – it is just that the acceptable way to say the word does not enable us to hear all the letters that are in it.

Look back at the sentence in the first paragraph –

'Many words have shorter words inside them.'

In a sentence containing only seven different words, there are these smaller words:

'man' is in **man**y   'short' is in **shor**ter

'any' is in m**any**   'or' is in sh**or**ter

'an' is in m**an**y

'or' is in w**or**ds

'word' is in **word**s

'ave' (avenue) is in h**ave**

'in' is in **in**side

'side' is in in**side**

'sid' is in in**sid**e

'the' is in **the**m

'hem' is in t**hem**

'he' is in t**he**m

The word 'the' is a common word and doesn't cause problems for too many people. Spotting it in '**the**m' will make 'them' easier to remember. The pattern 'ave' is commonly seen in addresses as a short form of 'avenue', so seeing it in 'h**ave**' will make that spelling memorable.

One of the smaller words in 'shorter' is 'short'. The 'er' is a suffix which has been added to change the way the word is used. When you come to the section on *Prefixes and suffixes* you will see how many words have extra bits stuck on the beginning or end of them to change their meaning or use.

Links

Sometimes you can easily pick out a link that the smaller word has with the meaning of the longer word. That will then help you to remember the spelling:

Please can I have a **pie**ce of **pie**.

If you **lie** to me I won't be**lie**ve you.

Add an **add**ress to your letter.

The **secret**ary will keep his **secret**.

Sometimes you can **make** the smaller word link with the long word by thinking up a new idea or image:

It is a **sin** to be in bu**sin**ess.

Her fat | her is **fat**.

Since I must **rely** on you, I am, **since** | **rely** yours.

To get her will mean that we can be **to** | **get** | **her**.

If you **rob** someone you have a p**rob**lem.

So, give **me so** | **me**!

You might have to **spit** when you are in ho**spit**al.

Listen while I say the **list**.

You are so **you**ng.

Be **sure** about your mea**sure**ments.

Her fat | **her** is **fat**.

Compound words

Some words are just two words joined together. They are called compound words and it is easy to see how they were formed. Recognizing compound words is useful, particularly when there is a silent letter involved. For instance, the word 'cupboard' sounds as though it could be spelt *cubburd. Noticing that it is actually 'cup' and 'board' will help you to remember it. (Was a cupboard originally a board with cups on it? Yes, and it dates back to about 1325 when it was 'a board or table to place cups and plates on'. In about 1530 the word's meaning altered to 'a closet or cabinet for food, etc'.)

Here are some examples:

tooth | paste – paste for a tooth

snow | man – man made out of snow

carry | cot – a cot which a person can carry

hose | pipe – a pipe which can be used to hose the plants

break | fast – time to break your overnight fast

news | paper – a paper containing news

flower | pot – a pot for a flower

finger | print – the print of a finger

hand | bag – a bag carried in your hand

Other words may not have been made deliberately by joining two words but they can still be broken into two:

set | tee

man | age

in | form

sup | port

Some words are made up of two bits that don't, at first, seem to make sense but if you know that

tele = at a distance

vision = to do with sight

then tele**vision** = seeing something which is coming from a distance

and **phone** = sound

then tele**phone** = sound coming from a distance

Understanding that

bi = 2

and **tri** = 3

gives us

bicycle = a cycle with 2 wheels

and **tri**cycle = a cycle with 3 wheels

Further examples

Here are some more examples of words within words. You could find others by looking in a dictionary.

au**die**nce	ass**is**tant
photo graphy	op**port unity**
realization	atmo**sphere**
camera	**prod**ucer
env**iron**ment	re**hear**sal
prob**able**	tri**angle**
funeral	cre**ate**
char acter	**dent**ist

Choosing a small word that you will remember

Some small words are more helpful than others. Look again at the word 'many'. There are three short words inside it:

an   man   any

If you want to learn to spell the word 'many', which do you think would be the most helpful? The words 'an' and 'any' are perhaps not as easy to remember as 'man' because you can attach a picture to 'man'. Using 'man', though, might leave you confused with the word 'men', because 'men' sounds like 'many'.

When you are working out how to break up your word, use a method that you will remember very clearly. You may have to use two or three memory levels to make sure that, in the months to come, you don't allow anything to confuse you. How about this sentence?

'**Any man** will do but there are too **many** to choose from!'

It uses both the small words and links to the meaning of the word as well.

General tip

It is important to work out which part of the word is the hard bit. If you already feel confident about the first few letters then don't spend time thinking about which method to use on them. Just look carefully at the tricky bit, which can often be in the middle of the word.

Activity

Find the smaller words in these words. (People's names, obscure words and words with only one letter are not included.)

1.	Monday	2 words
2.	computer	2
3.	really	3
4.	comfort	3
5.	football	3
6.	amateur	5
7.	tragedy	5
8.	choreography	6
9.	interesting	7
10.	knowledgeable	10

Answers are at the back of the book.

Prefixes and suffixes

You might have seen the word 'affix' on an envelope where it says:

AFFIX
STAMP
HERE

It is another word for 'stick'. In spelling, an affix is a group of letters you **stick** onto the front or back of the base part of a word. There are two types of affix:

A *prefix* sticks to the **beginning** of a base word. It will change the word's meaning:

PREFIX   BASE

un   +   happy   =   unhappy

'Unhappy' is the opposite of 'happy'.

A *suffix* sticks to the **end** of a base word to alter how it is used:

BASE   SUFFIX

comfort   +   able   =   comfortable

We might say –

'He was choosing a new chair and **comfort** was very important to him. The chair he chose was very **comfortable**.'

We wouldn't say 'The chair he chose was very **comfort**.' Suffixes help us to use words in different ways.

Spotting some of the common prefixes and suffixes will help you to break down words into smaller chunks. Some words can have a prefix and a suffix – (un)comfort(able). Some have more than one of each. One of the longest words in our language

antidisestablishmentarianism

is only a collection of prefixes and suffixes which have been stuck onto a base word:

PREFIX	PREFIX	BASE	SUFFIX	SUFFIX	SUFFIX
anti	dis	establish	ment	arian	ism

You can break down **establish** even further:

PREFIX	BASE	SUFFIX
e	stab**le**	ish

The 'e' at the end of 'stable' has to go because the suffix begins with a vowel. This will be explained later. (If you are unsure of what a vowel is, turn to the glossary at the back of the book.)

The whole word means 'The political position that is against the withdrawal of state recognition of an established church'. One student made this word using wooden letters on a very long table. Since then she has been an expert at spotting prefixes and suffixes!

Prefixes

The word 'prefix' is itself a good example of a word with a prefix. 'Pre' means before, so the prefix comes **before** the base word. Here are the meanings of some of our common prefixes:

pre = before	(pre)paid	=	paid beforehand
post = after	(post)-mortem	=	after death
inter = between	(inter)national	=	between nations
trans = across	(trans)atlantic	=	across the Atlantic
over = too much	(over)sleep	=	to sleep too long
uni = one	(uni)form	=	one outfit for one group
multi = many	(multi)storey	=	many levels
re = again	(re)play	=	to play again
de = to take away	(de)frost	=	to take away the frost
un = not	(un)fair	=	not fair
dis = not	(dis)agree	=	to not agree

Breaking up words

When you add a prefix to a base word, it will usually change the meaning of the word, as we have seen. The whole word then has an obvious meaning as above. Don't be put off if you see a prefix but you don't recognize or understand the rest of the word. It is still worth splitting it up. You will then only have to focus on spelling the rest of the word:

(ex)hale   (re)venge   (pre)pare   (de)tach   (uni)versal
(dis)gust

Prefixes usually just attach to the base word without needing any change of spelling. They can often be extremely helpful when remembering whether there is a double letter or not. For instance, (il), (im), (in) and (ir) are all prefixes which mean 'not'. Look at these words:

(il)legal   =   not legal

(im)moral   =   not moral

(in)numerate   =   not numerate

(ir)relevant   =   not relevant

When the base word begins with the same letter that ends the prefix:

il legal

you will know that you will have to have a double letter even though, of course, you can't hear two of them when you say the word.

Here are some more examples:

illogical	(il)logical	=	not logical
illicit	(il)licit	=	not licit – 'licit' is another word for legal
illegible	(il)legible	=	not legible
immobile	(im)mobile	=	not mobile
immature	(im)mature	=	not mature
immortal	(im)mortal	=	not mortal – somebody who is immortal will live for ever
irreplaceable	(ir)replaceable	=	not able to be replaced
irremovable	(ir)removable	=	not able to be removed

irregular	(ir)regular	=	not regular
irreversible	(ir)reversible	=	not reversible

Suffixes

ed	walk(ed)
ing	reply(ing)
s	table(s)
es	box(es)
able	accept(able)
ful	use(ful)
ment	arrange(ment)
less	hope(less)
ly	friend(ly)

Suffixes – changes in spelling

When a suffix is added, the spelling of the base word may change. This will depend on:

1. Which letter is at the end of the base word
2. Which letter is at the beginning of the suffix

It is helpful to be aware of why this happens but you can choose whether to learn the rule or to just learn the complete word. When you are in a panic and trying to spell a word, it is not easy to remember the rule. I have not attempted to cover everything about changing spellings when adding suffixes here but you can, of course, find out much more about these sorts of rules if they interest you.

These are the most common ways to add suffixes when you have to alter the spelling:

1. If the base word ends in an 'e' and you want to add a suffix beginning with a vowel, you normally drop the 'e'. This helps to keep the base word sounding as it should without changing any sounds. (When two vowels come together they can make a different sound. For instance, if 'based' was spelt without dropping the 'e' it would have to be said as 'bay-seed', which is not the same as 'base' with a /d/ sound on the end.)

mak**e** + ing	=	making
hop**e** + ing	=	hoping
car**e** + ing	=	caring
bas**e** + ed	=	based
argu**e** + ed	=	argued
determin**e** + ed	=	determined
intimidat**e** + ion	=	intimidation
educat**e** + ion	=	education
relat**e** + ion	=	relation
ador**e** + able	=	adorable
believ**e** + able	=	believable
debat**e** + able	=	debatable

Sometimes the letter 'e' stays if it is needed to help with the sound. Without keeping the 'e' in 'knowledg**e**able' we might try to pronounce the 'g' in the same way that we do at the end of the word 'mug'.

In the same way, we keep the letter 'e' in 'notic**e**able'. Otherwise we say 'cable' at the end of the word.

It would be easy to dive deeper into the rules here but we won't! The best thing is not to be surprised when you see a word which seems a bit strange. We do have many rules, each with a few or many exceptions. There are usually reasons for the exceptions, as in the examples above. You are probably already used to getting cross with our language and its oddities so the secret is not to get upset – just learn the word by breaking it up and don't worry about thinking of rules.

2. If the base word has a short sounding vowel before one consonant, then double the consonant:

run + ing	=	ru**nn**ing
cut + ing	=	cu**tt**ing
swim + ing	=	swi**mm**ing
stop + ed	=	sto**pp**ed

drip + ed	=	dri**pp**ed	
nod + ed	=	no**dd**ed	
big + est	=	bi**gg**est	
fat + est	=	fa**tt**est	
wet + est	=	we**tt**est	
win + er	=	wi**nn**er	
skip + er	=	ski**pp**er	

3. If the base word ends in 'y', the 'y' usually changes to 'i' before adding the suffix. This happens whether the suffix starts with a vowel or a consonant:

happ**y** + ness	=	happ**i**ness
heav**y** + ness	=	heav**i**ness
beaut**y** + ful	=	beaut**i**ful
pit**y** + ful	=	pit**i**ful
bab**y** + es	=	bab**i**es
arm**y** + es	=	arm**i**es
repl**y** + ed	=	repl**i**ed
occup**y** + ed	=	occup**i**ed
fur**y** + ous	=	fur**i**ous
glor**y** + ous	=	glor**i**ous
rel**y** + able	=	rel**i**able
env**y** + able	=	env**i**able
read**y** + ly	=	read**i**ly
prett**y** + ly	=	prett**i**ly

As you see, it can get confusing but there are plenty of words where the spelling **doesn't** change when you add a prefix or suffix. Look back at some of the words in this section. Lots of them have affixes. The following list of words from this section shows words which **do not** change their spellings when affixes are added:

    spell(ing)

    call(ed)

    type(s)

    change(s)

    mean(ing)

    small(er)

    chunk(s)

    long(est)

    collect(ion)

    be(ing)

    try(ing)

    add(ing)

This list shows words which **do** change their spelling:

spotting	=	spo**t** + ing	(double the last consonant)
easier	=	eas**y** + er	(change the 'y' to an 'i')
changing	=	chang**e** + ing	(drop the 'e')

Useful groups of words

Grouping together words which have the same base word can be very handy because an easy word can give a big clue to the spelling of a harder word:

    si**g**n – si**g**nal – si**g**nature

'Sign' is not easy to spell because we can't hear the 'g'. We can hear it in 'si**g**nal' and 'si**g**nature' though, so try to remember them together as a group.

    fin**i**te – infin**i**te – defin**i**te – defin**i**tely – indefin**i**tely

'Infinite' and 'definite' are difficult because the vowel sounds in the middle are not clear. They sound like *infanut and *defanut. Link it with the word 'finite' because the two /i/ sounds are very clear in that word.

heal – **heal**th – **heal**thy

The vowel sound in 'heal' changes to a different sound in 'health' and 'healthy'. Remembering that the base word is 'heal' will help you to spell the other two words.

mean – **mean**t – **mean**ing

Again, the vowel sound changes when a suffix is added. Link 'meant' with the other two words and you won't be tempted to spell it *ment.

know – **know**ledge

It is very easy to confuse 'know' with 'now'. Remember that 'know' is connected to the word 'knowledge'.

electri**c** – electri**c**ity – electri**c**ian

You can hear the /k/ sound at the end of 'electri**c**'. In the last two, the sound changes to /s/ so the spelling becomes harder. Think back to 'electric' if you need to write 'electricity' or 'electrician'.

gover**n** – gover**n**ment

It is hard to hear the 'n' in the longer word so link it with 'govern' and you will remember to include an 'n' when you spell 'government'.

resi**den**t – resi**den**t – resi**den**tial

You can hear 'den' clearly when you say 'resi**den**tial'. It isn't so clear in 'resi**den**t' though. Try to remember the connection between these two words.

General tip

During the day, when you see words around you, look out for small words inside long words, as well as prefixes and suffixes and you will be surprised at how many you find. You will soon get used to seeing words in a new way.

Activity

Put brackets around the prefixes and suffixes in these words:

1. unemployment
2. impolitely
3. dismembered
4. international
5. misunderstanding

Now write the base word of the following (and check the spelling in a dictionary):

6. writing
7. happiness
8. stopping
9. maker
10. coping

Match a prefix to each base word:

sub   dis   trans   tri   un

11. pleasant
12. angle
13. marine
14. action
15. appear

Answers are at the back of the book.

Say it oddly

Lots of our words are said the way they are written but there are plenty which aren't. When you are stuck with learning a word which has a silent letter or a strange spelling, try finding a different way to say it. Some of our letter combinations are so peculiar that you can easily make the word say something else which will stick in your mind.

Silent letters

Words with silent letters can be remembered by incorporating the silent letter into a new way of saying a word. For instance, we say 'Wednesday' as *Wens/day. We don't sound the 'd' or the second 'e' so try saying it oddly, so that you **can** hear those sounds:

The letter 't' is silent in 'mortgage' so say:

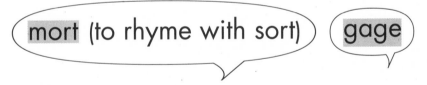

Several common words begin with 'wh', pronounced /h/. Try sounding out the 'w' on its own at the start of 'whose':

The silent letter in 'plumber' is 'b'. Attach it to the second half of the word so that you can hear it:

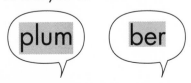

Say 'half' by pronouncing it with an 'h' in front of Alf:

Say 'scissors' by starting it in the same way as 'skin' or 'scarf':

Vowel pairs

The word 'friend' has a pair of vowels which doesn't fit into the normal pattern of sounds. Saying it oddly will remind you that the 'i' comes before the 'e':

The word 'miniature' also has two confusing vowels together. Separate the word and say:

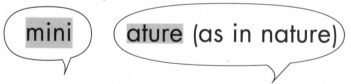

'Biscuit' sounds as though it should be spelt *biskit. So say it oddly:

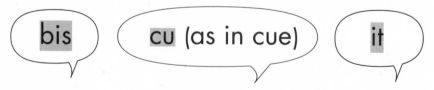

The 'ch' pair

We expect the letters 'c' and 'h' together to make a sound like the one that comes at the beginning and end of 'church'. However, when 'c' and 'h' sound like /k/ then it's not so easy to remember the spelling.

The word 'chemist' starts with a /k/ sound, so try saying it oddly, in the same way as you would start the word 'chat'. You could link a few of these words together:

> I go to the chemist to **ch**at about my stomach ache.

The letters in blue all sound like /k/ when you say them correctly. Say them *oddly* by saying them as you would say the bold letters.

Medical terms

Medical terms can be very tricky to spell. Let's look at some of them:

'eczema' sounds as though it should have an 'x' in it. Try saying it oddly by saying:

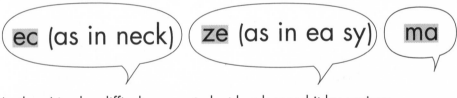

'asthma' is also difficult – one student has learned it by saying:

For 'bronchitis' she says:

Other words

Here are some other words which could be said oddly to help you remember the spelling:

answer   say   ans   wer (as in were)

February   say   Feb   ru (as in roo)   ary

division   say   di (as in die)   vision

police   say   pol   ice (as in ice)

machine   say   mach (as in macho)   ine (as in fine)

choreography   say   chore   o   graph   y (ee)

incapable   say   in   cap (as in headwear)   able

watch   say   watch (to rhyme with hatch)

picture   say   pic   ture

mechanic   say   me   chan   ic

discipline   say   disc   i   pline (to rhyme with fine)

hungry   say   (hun)   (gry (to rhyme with cry))

conscience   say   (con)   (science)

Activity

How would you break up these words to say them oddly?

1. knot
2. orchestra
3. massacre
4. crystal
5. usual
6. special
7. parliament
8. radiator
9. Thames
10. opinion

Answers are at the back of the book.

Syllables

This section is a very brief introduction to the world of syllables (say 'sill-a-bulls'). Finding syllables in words is one of the best ways to break up words if you are able to identify them. A syllable is one letter, or a group of letters, which forms part of a word. Sometimes it can be the whole word itself.

There are many ways of explaining it further. Choose the one that makes most sense to you. A syllable is:

a. A **beat** in a word. Think about beating time to a word on a drum. The number of beats in the word should be the same as the number of syllables.

b. A '**push**' of breath. Each syllable uses its own bit of breath as you breathe out.

c. A chunk of a word with **one vowel sound** in it.

d. The sound you make when you speak and your **jaw drops** down. Rest your chin on the back of your hand and feel each syllable when your jaw drops down on your hand.

All words can be broken into syllables. A word can contain one syllable, or several.

Vowels and consonants

Every syllable in every word must have at least a vowel, or a vowel sound. It would be very hard to actually say a word if we didn't use any vowels. Try saying **sd** or **trng** without adding any vowel sounds! The vowels help our mouths to move from one consonant sound to another.

The vowels are – **a e i o u**

b**a**g, b**e**d, p**i**t, t**o**p, m**u**st

The consonants are – **b c d f g h j k l m n p q r s t v w x z**

The letter 'y' can act as a vowel or a consonant. When it acts as a vowel it can sound like an 'i' as in 'fl**y**', an 'e' as in 'happ**y**' or /i/ as in 'tr**y**st'. When it acts as a consonant it sounds like the start of the word '**y**esterday'. It might be helpful to think of consonants as the sounds we make when using our lips, tongue or teeth. Say the word 'yesterday' and feel your tongue moving against the roof of your mouth at the beginning.

Two vowels together will often make one longer vowel sound:

sl **ee** p   p **ai** d   n **oi** se

A vowel and a consonant together can also make a longer vowel sound:

c **ar**   n **ow**   b **ir** d

Say the words above slowly and listen for the vowel sound in each one.

Numbers of syllables

The number of syllables in a word will usually equal the number of vowel sounds in a word.

sk**i**p	=	1 syllable	1 vowel sound
p**a**/per	=	2 syllables	2 vowel sounds
u/ni/ted	=	3 syllables	3 vowel sounds
in/tel/lig/ent	=	4 syllables	4 vowel sounds
h**i**p/p**o**/p**o**t/**a**m/**u**s	=	5 syllables	5 vowel sounds

Go back to the four descriptions of a syllable and check that the one that made sense to you works with the words above:

a. A beat in a word – use your pencil or pen to beat time to each word.

b. A 'push' of breath – say the word and focus on your breathing.

c. A chunk of a word with one vowel sound in it – try to hear each vowel sound when you say the word.

d. What you say when your chin drops on your hand – put your hand under your chin and let your chin rest on the back of your hand. Now say the words clearly and in an exaggerated way. Each time you open your mouth your jaw will drop down and that movement will equate to one syllable.

So you can see that dividing words into syllables depends a lot on seeing where the vowels are. Dividing the words so that each bit has a vowel in it will help you to say the separate bits and remember the spellings.

| den/tist | fi/nal | trav/el |
| per/haps | la/bel | shad/ow |

Some people will wonder exactly where to split the word. In many ways it doesn't matter. As long as each chunk contains one vowel, or one vowel sound, you will be able to remember the word in separate syllables. There are very few words in the English language which contain a syllable without a vowel sound.

Types of syllable

This section will not give you all the information about syllables because there is a lot to learn. However, you don't need to know it all before you can break up words into syllables. A brief look at some of the different types of syllable will show you what to look out for when you are deciding how to break up a word.

1. Open syllable: notice that there isn't a consonant at the end of the syllable. That is why it is called an open syllable and the vowel sound is allowed to go on.

The vowel says its name:

pa/per	listen for the 'a'
me/thane	listen for the 'e'
Ni/gel	listen for the 'i'
clo/thing	listen for the 'o'
u/nic/orn	listen for the 'u'

2. Closed syllable: in these syllables there is a consonant at the end of the syllable. It stops the sound going on and that is why it is called a closed syllable.

The vowel has a very short sound:

flat/ter	/a/ as in cat
pet/al	/e/ as in let
tip/ping	/i/ as in lip
lost	/o/ as in top
but/ter	/u/ as in must

3. Syllable where the vowel sound is made by two vowels together:

treat/ed

ac/count/ing

deg/ree

sham/poo

4. Syllable where the vowel sound is made by a vowel and a consonant together:

world

darl/ing

bird/song

show/er

5. Syllable where there is an 'e' at the end of it but it is not pronounced. Each of these syllables has another vowel in it which makes the vowel sound:

sen/tenc**e**

de/clin**e**

dic/tat**e**

corn/flak**e**

6. Syllable which comes at the end of a word and which can be found in many other words. It can be a suffix:

na/**tion**

pic/**ture**

walk/**ing**

music/**ian**

There are plenty of words which divide into syllables but which don't fit into any of the above categories. Just split the word where you think it makes sense to do so.

Remember SID.

Slowing it down will help you to identify the separate syllables in a word. For instance, when a student wanted to spell 'survive', she said it normally but wrote *surive with only one 'v'. She forgot to slow the word down and hear each separate syllable. If she had listened to herself say 'sur', then left a gap before the 'vive' bit, the first 'v' would have appeared when she spelt the word.

General tip

Important!
If this section on syllables doesn't make a lot of sense to you, then **don't worry**. Some people find it very hard to hear the different syllables in a word. Use the other methods when breaking up words. You will probably be quite good at using methods which rely on **seeing** the separate bits of words in your mind's eye, rather than hearing them. For instance, you will probably be able to use the *Small words* and *Word family* methods more easily than people who can use *Syllables* to break up a word.

Activity

Divide the following words into syllables. Don't worry if you don't manage to split them in exactly the right place. This is about helping you as an individual to learn the words and if you split the words in a way that helps you, then that's all that matters.

1. slogan

2. trumpet

3. joining

4. suburb

5. complete

6. option

Answers are at the back of the book.

Memory tricks

You have seen that your memory works best when you give it some assistance. This section will look at other ways of adding levels of memory in order to provide that help.

A memory trick will often double up with one of the other methods we have already looked at. Think back to the section on *Memory* which showed you how to remember the word 'separate'. There are small words in 'separate' but using the memory trick of visualizing the picture of the two rodents in your mind's eye would boost your memory of the word.

These memory tricks are often called 'mnemonics'. This is an odd spelling, but it comes from the Greek word 'mneme', which means 'memory'.

Pictures

Whenever possible, try to attach a picture to a difficult spelling. Your memory will store pictures better than almost anything else. Try saying the word out loud and use the first picture that comes into your mind.

One student wanted to be able to spell 'collect'. She found it hard to remember the second 'c'. Her first thought when saying the word was that she had **two** rubbish bins that needed collecting each week. She visualized a picture of two bins with the 'c's as their lids:

$$\text{c o l l e c t}$$

For some people, the letters 'b' and 'd' will often end up the wrong way round. Making a picture of a bed out of them will keep them the right way round:

$$\boxed{\text{b e d}}$$

You might remember that the word 'accommodation' has two 'c's and two 'm's if you picture a**cc**o**mm**odation with two **c**ots and two **m**attresses:

a c c o m m o d a t i o n

Here are some other pictures that could remind you of spellings.

s w a l l o w

heard

He h**ear**d it coming.

committee, coffee, settee

The spelling of 'surprise' was difficult for one student. He was happy with 'rise' and decided to use the meaning of it to make the whole word look different. He then only needed to concentrate on remembering the first four letters:

surp **rise**

First letters

Make up a saying. Use the letters of the difficult spelling as the first letters of words in your saying. 'Rhythm' is not an easy word to spell but it has a great saying to go with it:

Rhythm has your two hips moving!

Here are some other examples that might work for you:

beautiful	**wear**	**guilt**
b ig	**w** ear	**g** reen
e lephants	**e** arrings	**u** nderwear
a re	**a** nd	**i** s
u glier	**r** ings	**l** ess
t han		**t** empting
l		
ful		

souvenir	**daughter**	**because**
s old	**D** aisy	**b** e
o ver	**a** lways	**e** ver
U raguay	**u** ses	**c** areful
venir	**g** irly	**a** nd
	h airbrushes	**u** se
	ter	**s** harp
		e yes

Breaking up words

Only use this method if you feel confident about remembering the saying. If the meaning of the saying doesn't link with the meaning of the word, then you might struggle to remember it. Look at the examples above. The first five sayings each have a link with the word's meaning. The last one doesn't – being careful and using sharp eyes doesn't have much to do with the word 'because'. That doesn't mean to say that you wouldn't remember it; it will depend on how many memory levels you feel you need.

Try, also, to use this method when you only need five or six words in the saying. Otherwise, it might be too long to remember! You don't have to have a saying for the whole word – just the bit you find difficult:

daughter

beautiful

souvenir – one student found the first part hard, someone else might struggle with the last part

Make up a sentence

These will involve some thought. Once you have got into the way of breaking up words and seeing where the difficult bit is, you will find it easier to invent something which will be memorable.

It is necessary to have **one** collar and **two** sleeves in a shirt.

The CID investigates incidents and accidents.

If you are embarrassed you will have **two** red cheeks and **two** scarlet ears.

William K. Williams is an awkward boy.

Mathematics is easy.

Notice again how each sentence connects more or less with the meaning of the word. Each sentence should also give you an image which will aid your memory.

Silent letters sentences

Silent letters often cause problems. They are left over from a time when we used to pronounce them. You could make up a sentence with words starting with silent letters:

The knight knew the knack of knitting knickers.

I guessed the guitar was under guarantee.

The writer wrote about wrong wrinkles.

Whisper, don't whistle for the whisky at Whitsun.

You may already know how to spell one or two of the words. Perhaps you know that 'guitar' has a silent 'u' but you can't spell 'guarantee'. Putting them together means you are linking something new to something you already know.

General tip

Use colour as often as you can. For some people it will make a big difference. The bits of the words will stand out a lot more and have more impact. Use highlighters to make blocks of colour or separate pens for each letter.

Activity

1. Draw a picture to help you remember the spelling of 'parallel'.

2. Make up a saying using all, or some of, the letters of 'Britain'.

3. Fill in the missing word to complete this sentence: An island is ...

4. Make up a sentence using some of the following words. The letter 'b' is silent in each of them: lamb, comb, numb, thumb, crumb, tomb.

Suggestions are at the back of the book.

Word families

Two words that contain the same combination of letters in the same order are said to belong to the same word family. For example, the words 'n**ation**' and 'st**ation**' have '**ation**' in common, '**court**esy' and '**court**' have '**court**' in common and 'wh**irl**' and 'g**irl**' both have '**irl**' in them. You will see the same groups of letters repeated many times in different words. They won't always sound the same, which can lead to problems with their spellings. As adults you are likely to know the spellings of a good number of words. You can use this knowledge to your advantage by recognizing when you are struggling with a word that is in the same word family as one you **do** know.

You can make your own word families. There aren't any official word families – if you see the same letters, in the same order, in two or more different words then you can call that a word family.

For instance, you might be able to spell 'fence' but not 'independence'. So remember them as two words from the '**ence**' family. If you need a deeper level of memory then picture someone escaping from prison over a fence so that he can gain his independence.

> f**ence**, independ**ence**

Here are some more examples of words in the same word family:

che**que**, **que**ue	**sy**rup, **sy**ringe	**eve**ry, **eve**ning
sh**out**, h**ou**se	a**ffect**, in**fect**	for**eig**n, n**eigh**bours
br**own**, sh**ow**er	**pres**cribe, **pres**ent	n**one**, comp**one**nt
j**oin**, disapp**oin**t	br**other**, m**other**	**weight**, h**eight**
b**read**, d**read**ful	d**itch**, sw**itch**	fl**our**, col**our**

'ice' and 'ise'

> pract**ice**, adv**ice**
>
> pract**ise**, adv**ise**

Lots of people use the wrong 'practise/practice'. Americans only use the one with a 'c' so it's easy for them! We use the spelling 'pract**ise**' when we use it as a verb and say:

I am going to practise my speech.

I am practising my speech now.

Then we use it as a noun and say:

I enjoyed the practice at the football club this morning.

If it sounds confusing, then look at the words **before** 'practise/practice'. '**To** practise' gives you the clue that it's a doing word (verb). '**The** practice' tells you it's a noun. 'Practising' always has an 's' because it is always a verb.

Also, link them with 'advise' and 'advice'. It is easier to spot the difference between those two words because, when we say them, they **sound** different. 'Advise' is the verb:

I would like to advise you.

'Advice' is the noun:

Please take my advice.

Word families linked by meaning

Here are some more family groups of words linked by meaning.

All these words ask questions:

who, **wh**at, **wh**en, **wh**ere, **wh**y, **wh**ich

Remembering these together will help when you are not sure whether to use 'there' or 'their':

here, t**here** and everyw**here**

Choosing your words

Take care when choosing words to help you learn a spelling.

Someone wanted to learn to spell the word 'umbrella'. He knew the first six letters – *umbrel – but got stuck at the end. He had recently learned the word 'large' and wanted to link it with 'umbrella' to help him with the spelling. Can you work out why this would **not** have been a good idea?

u m b r e l l a
l a r g e

The first reason why this is not a good link is that 'large' has only one 'l' and 'umbrella' has two. So you might end up with:

*u m b r e l a

The second reason is that it sounds as though 'umbrella' might have the letter 'r' at the end of it, in the same way that 'large' has the letter 'r' after the 'a'. You might end up with:

*u m b r e l l a r

Either way it would be easy to make a mistake. The learner would be better off linking it with a word such as 'Stella', as long as he was happy with that spelling:

u m b r e l l a
S t e l l a

As well as having the same spelling pattern, the words 'umbrella' and 'Stella' also rhyme. He could use the sound of the rhyme to back up the visual impact of the pattern.

He could have made up a memory trick using the awkward letters as first letters of a memorable sentence:

umb

rain
ends
long
lightning
adventure

Finding word families

It can be difficult to think of another word belonging to the same word family as the word you want to learn to spell. Browse through a dictionary until you find one that contains the same group of letters, or try putting 'word families' into an internet search engine and seeing which groups of words appear.

On the next few pages, you will find lists of some word families.

Breaking up words

ack	ad	ail	ain	ake	ale	all
attack	bad	ail	brain	bake	bale	ball
back	cad	bail	gain	brake	dale	call
black	dad	email	grain	cake	female	fall
crack	fad	fail	main	flake	gale	hall
hack	had	hail	pain	lake	kale	mall
jack	lad	jail	plain	make	male	pall
knack	mad	mail	rain	quake	pale	stall
lack	pad	nail	stain	rake	sale	tall
pack	sad	pail	terrain	sake	shale	wall
quack	tad	quail	train	stake	stale	
rack		rail		take	tale	
sack		sail		wake		
smack		snail				
snack		tail				
stack		wail				
tack						
track						

am	ame	an	ank	ap	ash	at
cam	blame	an	bank	cap	ash	at
dam	came	ban	blank	chap	bash	bat
ham	dame	bran	clank	clap	cash	brat
jam	fame	can	crank	flap	clash	cat
pram	game	clan	flank	gap	crash	chat
ram	lame	fan	hank	lap	dash	fat
slam	name	flan	lank	map	gash	flat
tram	same	gran	plank	nap	hash	hat
wham	shame	plan	prank	rap	lash	mat
	tame	ran	rank	sap	mash	pat
		span	sank	scrap	rash	rat
		tan	tank	tap	sash	sat
				trap	slash	tat
					stash	that
						vat

Breaking up words

ate	aw	ay	eat	eel	eep	eet
ate	claw	away	beat	eel	beep	beet
crate	draw	bray	cheat	feel	cheep	feet
date	flaw	clay	eat	heel	deep	fleet
fate	gnaw	day	feat	peel	keep	greet
grate	jaw	delay	heat	reel	peep	meet
hate	law	hay	meat	wheel	sheep	sleet
late	paw	lay	neat		sleep	sweet
mate	raw	may	peat		steep	
plate	saw	pay	seat		weep	
rate	straw	play	wheat			
state		ray				
		say				
		spray				
		stay				
		sway				
		tray				
		way				

ell	en	ent	est	ice	ick	ide
bell	den	bent	best	dice	kick	bride
cell	fen	cent	jest	ice	lick	chide
dell	hen	dent	nest	lice	nick	hide
dwell	men	lent	pest	mice	pick	pride
fell	pen	rent	quest	nice	prick	ride
hell	ten	sent	rest	rice	quick	side
quell	wren	tent	test	slice	sick	slide
sell		vent	vest	twice	slick	tide
smell		went	west		stick	wide
spell					thick	
swell					tick	
tell					trick	
well					wick	

Breaking up words

ife	ight	ile	ill	in	ine	ing
knife	bright	bile	bill	bin	brine	bring
life	delight	file	hill	din	dine	cling
rife	fight	mile	ill	grin	fine	ding
strife	flight	pile	mill	in	line	fling
wife	fright	rile	pill	kin	mine	king
	light	smile	quill	pin	nine	ping
	might	stile	sill	shin	pine	ring
	night	tile	still	spin	swine	sing
	right	vile	till	thin	twine	sling
	sight	while	trill	tin	vine	spring
	slight		swill	twin		sting
	tight		will	win		string
	tonight					swing
						thing
						wing

ink	ip	it	oat	ock	og	oil
blink	blip	bit	bloat	block	bog	boil
brink	dip	chit	boat	chock	cog	broil
chink	grip	fit	coat	clock	clog	coil
ink	hip	grit	float	cock	dog	foil
link	lip	hit	gloat	dock	fog	oil
mink	nip	it	goat	flock	frog	soil
pink	pip	kit	moat	frock	hog	spoil
rink	ship	lit	oat	hock	jog	toil
shrink	sip	pit	throat	knock	log	
sink	slip	quit		lock	slog	
stink	tip	sit		mock	smog	
think	trip	spit		o'clock		
wink	whip	twit		rock		
		wit		sock		
		writ		stock		

Breaking up words

oke	oo	ood	oof	ook	ool	oom
awoke	boo	brood	goof	book	cool	bloom
bloke	goo	food	hoof	brook	fool	boom
broke	loo	good	proof	cook	pool	broom
coke	moo	hood	roof	crook	spool	doom
joke	too	mood	spoof	hook	stool	gloom
poke	zoo	stood		look	tool	loom
spoke		wood		rook		room
stroke				shook		zoom
woke				took		

oon	oop	oot	op	ope	ore	orn
boon	coop	boot	crop	cope	bore	born
buffoon	droop	coot	drop	dope	core	corn
goon	hoop	foot	flop	elope	chore	horn
moon	loop	hoot	hop	hope	fore	morn
noon	scoop	loot	mop	mope	gore	scorn
soon	snoop	root	pop	rope	lore	thorn
spoon	troop	scoot	stop	scope	more	
		shoot	top		ore	
		soot			pore	
		toot			score	
					sore	
					spore	
					store	
					tore	
					wore	

Breaking up words

ot	ought	ould	ouse	out	ow
blot	bought	could	douse	about	(rhymes with cow)
cot	brought	should	grouse	lout	bow
dot	fought	would	house	out	cow
got	ought		louse	pout	how
hot	sought		mouse	rout	now
jot	thought		spouse	shout	row
lot				spout	sow
not				stout	vow
plot					wow
pot					
rot					
shot					
spot					
tot					

ow	own	uck	ug	ump	unk
(rhymes with low)	brown	buck	bug	bump	bunk
blow	crown	duck	chug	dump	hunk
bow	down	luck	drug	hump	junk
crow	drown	muck	dug	jump	skunk
flow	frown	pluck	hug	lump	sunk
glow	gown	puck	jug	pump	trunk
grow	town	stuck	lug	rump	
low		tuck	mug	stump	
mow		yuck	plug	trump	
row			rug		
show			tug		
slow					
snow					
stow					
throw					
tow					

Activity

Think of, or find in a dictionary, some more words in the same family as:

1. pic**ture**, na**ture** and aper**ture**

2. h**air**, st**air**s and f**air**ly

3. mist**ake**, r**ake**d and l**ake**

4. ch**oice**, sp**oil** and **oint**ment

5. **str**ong, **str**aight and **str**ength

Suggestions are at the back of the book.

Test yourself

Now that you have looked at the six different ways of breaking up words you are nearly ready to start the four-week routine. Before you do that, test yourself with the following words and see if you can choose the best method for learning each word. You may come up with a different answer from the one at the back of the book but it doesn't matter, as long as you have chosen a method that would help you to learn the word. An explanation of why a particular method works with each word is given with the answers at the back of the book.

1. college – The difficulty is usually remembering the first 'e'. It is often spelt 'collage' which means something different – a collection of materials which have been stuck on to a backing board.

2. culminate – A long word which means to reach a point of highest development. There are a few small words in it but nothing significantly helpful. There is probably a better method to use.

3. rhyme – A bit like rhythm. Could you use the same method?

4. virtual – The vowels 'u' and 'a' are not sounded clearly when we say the word. What will help you to remember them?

5. medicine – Again, we don't sound out the middle letters. One of the problems with this word is that there is a /s/ sound in the middle of it as well.

6. kitchen – How can you remember that there is the letter 't' as well as the 'ch'?

7. gross – This could easily be muddled with the word 'grocer'.

8. unfortunately – A long word which lends itself to more than one method of remembering it. Which one would suit you?

9. season – Both the syllables in this word could be spelt in other ways. It could also be confused with the word 'cease'.

10. effectiveness – At first glance this looks confusing but if you can pull it apart it becomes much easier.

11. through – This word is often muddled with 'though' and 'thought'. How would you remember which is which?

12. anecdotal – A difficult one, but it can be done!

PART C

THE FOUR-WEEK ROUTINE

This part of the book is all about you improving your spelling over the next four weeks.

You will need to find half an hour or so on the first day when you start things off but, after that, you will need only two or three minutes each day for the rest of the week. Looking at your spellings should become a daily habit.

Start on any day of the week you choose – it doesn't have to be a Monday. If you work Monday to Friday, you could start the routine on a Sunday when you might have more time to sort out your list of new words to learn. Then you will be testing yourself the following Sunday. You will need a notebook and some highlighter pens.

The four-week routine

WEEK ONE – Monday

1. Think of a word you often want to use but always get wrong. Find the correct spelling of the word by using a dictionary, asking someone or taking it from a book. This is very important as it is too easy to learn the wrong spelling.

2. On the first page of the notebook write today's date at the top. Then write the word you have chosen clearly, under the date. Check that you have each letter in the right order.

> 19th May
>
> *Friend*

3. Look at the word carefully. Take your time. Decide which is the hard bit. It might be the whole word which is difficult.

Is there a *Small word* inside?

Does it have a *Prefix* or a *Suffix*?

Could you *Say it oddly*?

Can you break it into *Syllables*?

Is there anything in the word that makes you think of a *Memory trick*?

Does it belong to a *Word family*?

4. Decide how you are going to break up the word. Draw lines to divide it into chunks. Colour each bit with a different highlighter pen or just highlight the difficult area. If, at first, you are not sure how to break it up you could try different options on some rough paper. You could also try writing the word on strips of card and using scissors to decide where to make the breaks.

5. Think about the method, or methods, you are going to use to help you to remember it:

- Are there enough memory layers?
- Have you split the word so that you have about three letters in each bit? (Don't leave one letter on its own unless it's really helping you.)
- Have you thought about using another sense?

6. Say the word out loud slowly to help you hear the different parts of it. Not all words can be said as they are spelt but it is useful to say and hear the words which are.

Remember SID.

7. Cover the word with your hand or a piece of paper. **See** the word clearly in your mind's eye. If you don't have a clear picture, then uncover the word and have another look.

It is important that you do the next step (**Write**) with a picture of the word in your mind if at all possible.

You may have such a clear picture that you can say the letters of the word backwards.

If you can do that, then you are getting very close to fixing the word in your memory!

If that is very difficult for you, then just concentrate on getting the **sounds** of the word running through your mind in the right order from the beginning of the word.

Remember to cover the word before going on to the next step.

8. Write it just beside the original word.

9. Check to see if it is right. If it is right give it a tick. If it is wrong put a **x** beside it and think about why it was wrong.

- Were there too many letters in each bit?
- Did you use the best method? You might need to look at a different one.
- Was the memory layer deep enough?

Now find four other words. Add them to the same page and go through the same routine. Later you can choose to do more than five each week if you want but this is a good number to start with.

If it is hard to think of words you can't spell, then try some of the following:

- Write as much as you can about yourself and ask someone you trust to find the spelling mistakes.

- Look at any printed text in your workplace and pick out words you find difficult.

- If you are a student on a course, look in your textbooks.

- Look in newspapers or magazines.

- Borrow an audio book from the library. Play the tape and write what you hear. (You will have to pause it often.) Then check what you have written with the page in the book.

- Use the word list at the back of this book.

Tuesday

On the next day, write the date at the top of the next page and follow this routine with all your words:

Remember SID.

Look – Look back to where you wrote the word yesterday and remind yourself of how you broke it up. Run through the method or methods you have chosen.

Say – Hearing the sounds will help.

Cover – **Don't copy**, it won't help! Try to picture it in your mind's eye or hear the separate sounds.

Write – Join the letters if you can. (See the section on *Cursive writing*.)

Check – Give each word a tick or a cross.

Wednesday to Saturday

Follow the same routine for the rest of the week. Each day, make sure you are looking back to where you wrote the word for the first time. Don't rely on what you wrote the day before because that will not show you the coloured parts of the word or how you split it up.

Sunday

Test yourself! Try all five words but don't look at them first. If there is someone else who could test you, ask them. It is always good to involve someone else if you can.

The first couple of pages of your notebook should look a bit like this:

3rd Aug		4th Aug	5th Aug
slight night	slight ✓	slight ✓	slight ✓
(fri) (end)	friend ✓	friend ✓	friend ✓
irrelevant ir + relevant	irrelevant ✓	irrelevant ✓	irrelevant ✓
car / toon loon	carton ✗	cartoon ✓	cartoon ✓
young You are so young.	young ✓	young ✓	young ✓

In the example above, the word 'cartoon' was spelt incorrectly on the first attempt. It might have been because it was the first chunk that was highlighted – 'car' – as a small word, and the second bit was ignored. Something else was needed to help with 'toon'. It is fine to go back and add another strategy if necessary. In this case the double 'o' was the problem so it was linked with 'loon'.

Take some time to think about how well the routine worked for you. Which methods were the best? Which words have you learned really well?

WEEK TWO – Monday to Saturday

Follow the same routine as you did last week but with five new words. If you found five was not enough last week, then you could increase the number to six or seven this time. It is a good idea to make ten the maximum if you feel you can cope, but it is better to increase the number by one each week, rather than go straight up to ten.

If you found it hard to cope with five, go down to two or three. You can always build up again later.

Sunday

Test your words from this week. If you are getting them right – very well done!

Then, check last week's words – without looking at them first, if you can remember what they are. Or ask someone else to test you if you can.

If you are not able to ask anyone to help and have forgotten what the old words were, you could use a tape recorder, or some form of recording equipment. Record the old words and play them when you want to test yourself.

If you have followed the routine each day you should now be able to spell about ten words that you couldn't spell before.

If you are looking at the words each day and still not getting them right, then you may need to look again at Parts A and B. You may have chosen some words that confuse you because they are **nearly** the same. It's best not to have words like

n**ei**ghbour   and   n**ie**ce

in the same list, or

th**ere**   and   th**eir**

Make sure you put them in different lists. Keep a separate note of the words you want to learn in the future so that you don't forget them.

It would be helpful to include words in the same list from the same *Word family* or with the same base word, though. You could have **tool** and sch**ool** in the same week, or **know** and **know**ledge.

WEEK THREE

Follow the same routine as you did for weeks one and two. On Sunday test yourself on the words from **all three** weeks.

By now you should be well into the routine of spending two or three minutes each day going through your words. The more you are able to actually use them during the day the more they will stick. It is important to pick words that you will use often.

In order to find words to learn, some people like to keep a diary. They write about what they have done during the day. Again, you will need someone to read it for you to check for mistakes – these will show you which words you need to learn.

WEEK FOUR

This week you will be choosing your fourth set of words. You may find that you are using the same method of splitting up the words each time. If that works for you then that's fine. It is important to try out all the strategies though, because not all words can be learned by using just one method of breaking them up. Remind yourself of the other methods by looking back at Part B.

At the end of this week you should be able to spell words you could not spell four weeks ago. You should also feel more confident about learning to spell words in the future. As the weeks go by you will obviously be collecting a lot of new words. You will probably not want to test yourself on all of them every week. Take off the list the ones that you are completely sure of and only leave the harder ones on the list for testing each week.

Remember that:

- The success of the routine depends upon looking at the word, and the way it has been broken up, each day for at least a week.

- The more often you use the word, the more likely you are to remember how to spell it.

- Breaking a word into smaller chunks is the key to learning it.

PART D

THINGS YOU SHOULD KNOW ABOUT SPELLING

This part of the book covers subjects which will be of interest to anyone who wants to improve their spelling.

Homophones

Homophones are words that sound the same but are spelt differently:

homo = same   phone = sound

There are over 600 pairs or triplets of words in our language that sound the same. Thankfully, we only use about 50 of them on a regular basis but there are enough of them in use to cause us a few problems.

It is not uncommon to see the wrong one used in books and magazines etc. As mentioned before, 'practise' and 'practice' are often used wrongly. Another very common error is the misuse of 'complement' and 'compliment'. (See below for an explanation.) You can learn how to spell homophones in the same way as you would learn any other word but the problem is remembering which one to use when. The trick is to make sure that you link the word to something which will help you with the meaning.

For instance, the word 'new' sounds like the word 'knew'. The first one means the opposite of old, the second one is to do with having knowledge. So you could link 'knew' with 'know' and 'knowledge'. Perhaps you could say something like:

He knew all about kings and queens and had a great knowledge of history.

Then you have not only linked 'knew' with 'knowledge' but have added in the word 'king' which begins with the letter 'k' and gives you another memory layer.

You don't necessarily have to think of something to help you remember 'new' because, if you can remember the sentence above, you will automatically know when to use 'new' – when it isn't anything to do with knowledge!

Let's look at some of the homophones which cause the most problems:

Things you should know about spelling

to	two	too
their	there	they're
it's	its	
whether	weather	
which	witch	
by	buy	
where	wear	

Try this short quiz to see which ones you need to practise:

Activity

Circle the correct homophone.

1. The **two/to/too** boys were asked if they wanted **two/to/too** come to the football match **two/to/too**.

2. **They're/their/there** off on **they're/their/there** holidays tomorrow and will be travelling **they're/their/there** by car.

3. **It's/Its** nearly Autumn and time for the tree to shed **it's/its** leaves.

4. They will decide **whether/weather** they go or not when they see what the **whether/weather** is like.

5. There was more than one **which/witch** at the Hallowe'en party but it was difficult to say **which/witch** one had the best costume.

6. The picture had been painted **by/buy** a famous artist but the man did not have enough money to **by/buy** it.

7. She had just bought a new dress but didn't know **where/wear** she would be able to **where/wear** it.

8. After his football **practise/practice** he decided to **practise/practice** riding downhill on his skateboard.

9. The woman from the council has given permission to **license/licence** the new wine bar and will send the owners an alcohol **license/licence** later in the week.

Answers are at the back of the book.

Here are some suggestions for remembering any you got wrong in the exercise:

to – if in doubt, use this spelling – it is the most common

two – 2 (as in **tw**ice, **tw**ins, **tw**elve, **tw**enty)

too – more than you need, 'too much', 'too many' (think of this word as having one more letter 'o' than 'to' – one 'o' too many)

too – as well (imagine each letter 'o' as someone's face – they are coming with you as well)

their – a group of people own something (**heir** to the throne, the throne is **their**s)

there – **here**, **there** and every**where**

they're – they **a**re (the apostrophe shows that a letter is missing)

it's – it **is** (the apostrophe shows that a letter is missing)

its – belonging to it or part of it, for example, In Autumn the tree sheds its leaves. (Does the same job as 'her' and 'his', which do not have apostrophes – The girl lost her coat. The boy dropped his ball.)

whether – a word used to show a doubt or a choice (link it with all the other '**wh**' words which often ask a question – see below)

we**at**her – rain, sun, wind, snow etc (you can only **eat** outside in good we**at**her)

which – can be the start of a question (think of all the other words that start questions and begin with **wh** – **wh**at, **wh**en, **wh**y, **wh**at, **wh**o)

w**itch** – a w**itch** might have an **itch** from sitting on a broomstick!

by – if in doubt, use this one – it is the most common

bu**y** – use this when something costs money (think of the letter '**u**' as an open purse with no money left in it)

where – **Wh**ere is it? It's **here**!

wear – ladies w**ear** **ear**rings on each **ear**

By the way, the correct uses of compliment and complement, and complimentary and complementary, are as follows:

He paid her a compliment by telling her how pretty she looked.

The secretary included a compliments slip in the envelope when she sent the brochure to a client.

The famous pop star sent complimentary tickets to his family so that they could see his concert for free.

The full complement of the ship was 10 officers and 60 sailors.

Homoeopathy is considered to be alternative medicine, sometimes known as a complementary treatment.

Be careful when learning homophones. To avoid confusion, don't learn both of a pair at the same time. Do one this week and the other a couple of weeks later and, remember, use a memory trick to link a part of the word with something connected with its **meaning**.

Cursive (joined-up) handwriting

There are good reasons for joining up the letters when you write. It should make your writing look neat and mature but it will also help you to remember spellings.

Going back to what was said earlier, as well as having a visual memory and an auditory memory, we also have a motor memory. This is to do with movement. Our muscles can 'remember' shape and movement so that when we write a word, they will form an imprint of the flow and pattern of the letters. We can't use this motor memory as a spelling aid if all the letters are printed separately, without any flow.

General tip

If you are not sure of the differences in the names of letters, the following will help.

Small letters means the same as **lower case letters**: abcdefghijklmnopqrstuvwxyz

Capital letters, **upper case** and **block letters** all mean the same thing: ABCDEFGHIJKLMNOPQRSTUVWXYZ

Here are a few tips if you want to try a cursive style:

1. Capitals should always be on their own and not joined.

E ngland

2. Each small letter has an entrance stroke and an exit stroke.

3. Each small letter starts the entrance stroke on the line.

4. Most small letters are half the size of the capitals. It is important to get the size right as that will affect the look of a word.

a A   b B   c C   d D   e E   f F

g G   h H   i I   j J   k K   l L

m M   n N   o O   p P   q Q

r R   s S   t T   u U   v V

w W   x X   y Y   z Z

Joining some letters can be tricky. Be careful with **o**, **r**, **v** and **w** as they all have their exit strokes coming away at the top of the letter.

o   r   v   w

Try copying these:

carpet   button   review

vile   wash   worry

road

5. You may feel that you need all the help you can get with your spelling, so give the cursive style a go for a while to see whether you think you could change.

Don't forget, the most important thing about your writing is that it can be read easily. If your writing is legible and it looks better without being joined, then it's fine to stick with it. Changing your writing style will be hard as it can mean changing some very old habits.

Capital letters

Before printing was done by machines, all documents were created by hand. The printer had a set of metal letters, and would pick out letters to be put together, covered with ink, and pressed onto paper. Individual letters were kept in separate boxes, and displayed on a wooden stand. The individual capital letters were kept in the **UPPER CASE** on the stand, and the small letters were kept in the **lower case**. We now refer to capitals as 'upper case letters'. Sometimes you will also see the words 'block letters', particularly on forms.

Some adults develop a habit of using only capital letters (upper case) when they write. There are different reasons for this. Some people say that they find it easier than using lower case letters. Some people have even said to me that they find it quicker. In some cases they have mistakenly thought that it would be helpful for their young children to see and have carried on using it even though their children have grown up and developed their own cursive style.

You might have developed this habit because you found that it helps with your spelling. This is because some letters that are easily confused as small letters have quite different shapes as capitals. For instance, the letter 'b' and the letter 'd' are mirror images of each other and it can be hard to remember which one to use, but the capital versions – 'B' and 'D' – are not. Again, 'p' and 'q' are similar but their capitals – 'P' and 'Q' – are different.

If the people who read your writing are not people you need to impress, or it really doesn't matter if you use capitals or not, then you may just want to carry on using them. Of course, we are often told to use capitals, or block letters, when filling in forms, so an 'all capitals' style may have developed from having to complete lots of these. If you have done this for many years it could be a difficult habit to break. It is worth a try as you may find it easier than you think and, as you will see below, there is a big advantage to be had by using both upper and lower case.

Visual memory

As I have mentioned before, some people find it easier to remember the words by their look rather than their sound. The look of a word is partly determined by its overall shape. As you saw in the section on *Memory*, each word has its own, almost unique, shape when written in lower case. If you write a word using just capitals, that shape is not very different from any other word:

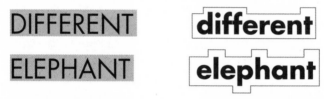

DIFFERENT **different**

ELEPHANT **elephant**

Changing your style

Have a look at two samples of writing by someone who decided to change their style:

> One day as I was walking down Prege I head the sound of troting. I tund and walked behand me a shagey dark hair of a fritend little hovers. I surch in my pocket for a apple from my dinner to give to him. I no were you Too t Shod be I said. So I removed the Belt of my rain Cote and tied it arowed his neck and led him Back back. I opened the great. Gete and satisfashon he gallaped in to hes filed. I was Sertly very happy and now that he was self self away from the darges traffic.

> One day, as I was walking down Bridge Street, I heard the sound of trotting. I turned and saw behind me the shaggy dark hair of a frightened little horse. I searched in my pockets for an apple from my dinner to give to him. 'I know where you should be', I said. So I removed the belt of my raincoat and tied it around his neck and led him back. I opened the gate, and with satisfaction he galloped into his field. I was certainly very happy now that he was safe, away from the noisy and dangerous traffic.

By the way, her spelling improved too!

As you become more confident about your spelling you will want your writing to look better so that you can show off your new skills. You won't want to make your writing small and messy so that the reader can't tell if the word is right or wrong.

Activity

Try copying some of the words below. If you are keen to have a go then there are plenty of books which will give you more hints and practice. Write your name and address in a cursive style as well.

London   Portsmouth

Leeds   York

Wales   England

Scotland   Ireland

Monday   Tuesday

Wednesday   Thursday

Friday   Saturday

Sunday

tomorrow   today   yesterday

morning   afternoon

I am practising a cursive handwriting style.

Letter name spelling

As you already know there are a lot of words which are not spelt as they sound. Even if they are spelt as they sound, there is often a tricky decision to make when there is a choice of letters to represent those sounds. Letter name spelling is usually very helpful for those words which are irregular and defy all other attempts to learn them! It should really only be used for a few, awkward words as it would be quite difficult to use all the time – you will see why.

This method relies on using the names of letters (such as 'a', 'b' and 'c') and has nothing at all to do with the sounds. Many of you will have been told not to use the names of letters when you are helping your children. That is correct because it is important for young children to concentrate on phonics, or whatever method they are learning at school. As an adult, however, you can use this method for words that are proving troublesome, even after you have tried all six methods of breaking the word up.

Some of you will have tried to learn spellings by writing words over and over again. You may have been told to do this at school, because copying a word many times will, for some people, ensure that it is anchored in the visual memory. If you were also using a cursive, or joined-up, handwriting style then you will have been using your motor memory as well. Unfortunately, although it is a good idea in principle, many people need to do more than just copy the word 20 or 30 times.

I have already mentioned how important it is to use as many different types of memory as possible. Using this method will involve your motor memory, your visual memory and your auditory memory. You will need a pencil and some paper.

1. Think of a word which you still struggle to spell – not a very long one. A word with between four and seven letters would be a good choice.

2. Find the correct spelling by using a dictionary or asking someone you trust.

3. Print the word on a piece of paper. Don't make it too small – it should be quite large. Separate each letter and give yourself the space to write over each letter several times:

r o u g h

4. Say each of the letter names – not the sound.

5. Now, say the letter name and, **at the same time**, write over the first letter. Repeat that for each letter in the word.

6. Go through the whole word, saying the letter name and writing the letter at the same time. Repeat this at least ten times.

7. Now, if you feel confident, join up the printed letters with entrance and exit strokes so that it looks like a cursive, or joined up, style. (See the section on *Cursive writing*.) Remember to say the letter name at the same time as you actually write it. Stick with just printing each letter if you prefer.

rough

Sometimes, it can be difficult to co-ordinate what you're saying with what you're writing. This method won't work as well as it could if you aren't careful to make sure you say the letter's name at the same time as you are writing it.

8. Repeat this step at least five times.

9. When you feel ready, cover what you have already written. Find a clear space on the page and write the word, saying the letter names again as you write it. You can print it or use a cursive style.

Every so often, over the next few days, remember to write the word and say each letter out loud as you do it. You will find that your auditory memory will help you with the letter order. You can see that you might get in a muddle if you do this with several words but it is worth remembering this method if you get completely stuck.

Neurolinguistic programming

There is another, similar method which relies on naming the letters in the word. It doesn't, however, involve your motor memory but instead it taps into what you could call your emotional memory. Learning to spell by using neurolinguistic programming, or NLP, can be very helpful for some people. Again, this is a method you might like to try for some of those very awkward words. It will be particularly useful if you have a strong visual memory and react well to seeing the word broken up into coloured chunks. I will briefly describe the method.

Spelling by NLP

Firstly, you need to recall a good emotional experience and a bad emotional experience. Make a note of where your eyes move to when you remember something good, and where you look when you recall the bad feeling. If, for instance you look up and to the left when you are thinking of something good, then that is where to look when you are focusing on the word you want to learn.

It is important to be in the right frame of mind and to be able to link the feeling that you have from a good emotional experience with spelling the word correctly. The word that you want to learn is then written on a card. It is split into two or three sections, each of which is written in a different colour.

opportunity

The card is then held in front of you in a position which was determined when you evoked the positive emotional memory. You then look at the card, visualizing and remembering each chunk of the word at a time. The card is hidden from you while you keep that picture in your mind. Eventually you are asked to recite the letters in the word, chunk by chunk. You are also asked to say the letters in the word backwards, as well as forwards! This is to ensure that you have a very clear picture of the word in your mind. If you do have that clear picture you should be able to say the letters backwards.

As you can see, this method is probably best done with someone else helping you. It could be adapted for use by one person but you will have to judge whether you feel that it would be of benefit to you. You would also need a greater understanding of how the NLP system works before you embark on this method.

Things you should know about spelling

Phonics

I have heard many people say that when they are not sure how to spell a word, they spell it the way it sounds. By doing that, you will probably be on the right track as the majority of our words **are** spelt as they sound. You might be relieved to know that only 14% of words are what we call irregular and can't be sounded out (such as 'island' or 'cough'), the other 86% are regular and **are** spelt as they sound. Of course, this isn't as easy as it appears because, as you know, there is often more than one way to spell a sound.

Phonics is a method of learning to read and spell by matching letters to sounds and sounds to letters. An understanding of phonics can help with the spelling of regular words. You might not have come across a word before but, if it is regular, then you stand a good chance of being able to work it out. For instance, you might never have seen the word 'chitterling', but you can read it (and possibly even be able to spell it) because you will recognize bits of the word:

ch as in **ch**urch   **itter** as in l**itter**   **ling** as in fal**ling**

Not everybody will be able to identify the different sounds within a word though, so if it is absolutely impossible for you, then don't keep trying. You may find that just using visual strategies such as *Small words*, *Memory tricks* and *Word families* will be enough. Some people with dyslexia will always find it difficult to distinguish some sounds. (See the section on *Dyslexia* for more information.)

However, it is certainly worth having a go. Try to identify the different, separate sounds that are in each word. Knowing what sound each letter, or combination of letters, represents will make a difference. Once you have got the hang of the different spelling choices for each sound, then it will be a lot easier.

Recently there has been a debate over which type of phonics is preferable – synthetic or analytic. Synthetic phonics involves learning the sounds that each letter represents and building them up to form words. Analytic phonics, on the other hand, looks at the words first and analyses the sounds that are in each word by breaking the word down. Schools are now being asked to teach children using synthetic phonics. If you have young children you will find that they are learning phonics at school so you can have a look at how they are doing it. By helping them you will be helping yourself at the same time.

It doesn't really matter which way you want to approach it. All that really matters is that, if you are interested in understanding a bit more about the sounds that make up our language, then it is worth attempting to hear them.

Remember SID.

Listen to the word 'string'. If you say it normally your brain might not be able to process sounds efficiently enough for you to identify each separate consonant at the beginning, and you could end up writing 'sting' or 'sing'. But if you slow it down, each sound stands a chance of being heard and identified so that you can spell it accurately.

The 44 sounds in our language, or phonemes, are listed below with some of the spelling choices for each sound.

/a/	pat	/g/	gate, egg, ghost
/ae/	ape, baby, main, steak, neighbour	/h/	hat, whole
/air/	hair, mare, bear	/j/	jet, giant, cage, bridge

Things you should know about spelling

/ar/	j**ar**, f**a**st	/l/	**l**ip, be**ll**, samp**le**, pupi**l**
/e/	m**e**t, h**ea**d	/m/	**m**an, ha**mm**er, co**mb**
/ee/	sw**ee**t, m**e**, p**ea**ch, pon**y**	/n/	**n**ut, di**nn**er, **kn**ee, **gn**at
/i/	p**i**g, want**e**d, c**y**gnet	/ng/	ri**ng**, si**n**k
/ie/	k**i**t**e**, w**i**ld, l**igh**t, fl**y**	/p/	**p**an, ha**pp**y
/o/	l**o**g, w**a**nt, bec**au**se	/kw/	**qu**een
/oe/	b**o**n**e**, s**ou**l, b**oa**t, sn**ow**	/r/	**r**at, che**rr**y, **wr**ite
/oi/	c**oi**n, b**oy**	/s/	**s**un, dre**ss**, hou**se**, **c**ity, mi**ce**
/oo/	b**oo**k, w**ou**ld, p**u**t	/sh/	**sh**ip, mi**ssi**on, sta**ti**on, **ch**ef
/or/	f**or**k, b**a**ll, s**au**ce, l**aw**	/t/	**t**ap, le**tt**er, de**bt**, dropp**ed**
/ow/	d**ow**n, h**ou**se	/th/	**th**rush
/u/	pl**u**g, gl**o**ve, t**ou**gh	/th/	**th**at
/ur/	b**ur**n, p**er**son, w**or**k, b**ir**d	/v/	**v**et, slee**ve**
/ue/	tr**ue**, m**oo**n, scr**ew**, s**ou**p	/w/	**w**et, **wh**eel

/b/	boy, rabbit	/ks/ /gz/	box, exist
/c/ /k/	cat, key, duck, school, unique	/y/	yes
/ch/	chat, match	/z/	zip, fizz, sneeze, is, cheese
/d/	dog, ladder, rubbed	/zh/	treasure, Asia, azure
/f/	fat, cuff, photo, rough	/uh/	button, computer, doctor

Don't forget that some sounds need only one letter to represent them but others will need two, three or even four letters:

The sound at the beginning of 'egg' needs the one letter – 'e'

The sound that we say at the beginning of 'chip' needs two letters – 'c' 'h'

The sound in the middle of 'feel' needs two letters – 'e' 'e'

The sound in the middle of 'would' needs three letters – 'o' 'u' 'l'

The sound at the end of 'though' needs four letters – 'o' 'u' 'g' 'h'

It is important to remember that our language and our alphabet were not created at the same time or in the same place. We have ended up with an alphabet consisting of 26 letters but these letters need to represent the 44 different sounds that we use when we speak. So, you can see that it became necessary for each letter to do more than just one job.

Have a look at the following examples and see if you can hear the different sounds that are present in each word. Slow the words right down as you say them and identify each separate sound.

Things you should know about spelling

Remember SID.

at	a	t					2 sounds
cat	c	a	t				3 sounds
scat	s	c	a	t			4 sounds
scatter	s	c	a	tt	er		5 sounds
scattered	s	c	a	tt	er	ed	6 sounds
yesterday	y	e	s	t	er	d	ay	7 sounds
church	ch	ur	ch				3 sounds
churchyard	ch	ur	ch	y	ar	d	6 sounds

If you find it hard to identify each of the separate sounds, watch yourself saying the words in a mirror. Your mouth will change position every time you say a new sound. It may be a very small movement but you should be able to see it and feel it. If two letters together stand for one sound, your mouth won't change position.

Look back at the table showing the 44 different sounds. You can see that each sound can be represented in different ways. It is also worth being aware of how each letter can do many jobs. The letter 'e' is one that has more than most. Let's look at what it is doing in some words:

1.	mak**e**	Not sounded at all. It affects the sound the letter 'a' makes though.
2.	p**e**t	Makes the sound we hear at the beginning of 'egg'.
3.	br**ea**d	As 2 but needs the 'a' with it.
4.	f**ee**t	Two 'e's together sound like the letter's name.
5.	f**ie**ld	As 4 but needs an 'i' with it instead.
6.	r**ea**l	As 4 but needs the 'a' with it instead.
7.	P**e**t**e**	The second 'e' is making the first one sound like its name!
8.	n**eigh**bour	Together with the 'igh' it is making the sound at the beginning of the word 'acorn'.
9.	n**ear**	Together with the 'ar' it makes the sound that we hear in the word 'ear'.

Equally we can look at one sound and see the different ways it can be spelt. All the following words have the same sound in them:

1. thr**ow**
2. s**ew**
3. st**o**ne
4. th**ough**
5. t**oe**
6. **o**ver
7. b**oa**t

So, when you hear the sound /o/ you have to choose which letter or letters you need. Thankfully, your visual memory will come into play as you will often be able to work out which one looks right.

Things you should know about spelling

Silent letters

Most of the letters in the alphabet can be silent in some words – there are only five which are always sounded:

f, **j**, **q**, **v** and **x**

Activity

Look at these words and try to identify the silent letter in each one. The answers are at the back of the book.

lamb

Wednesday

kneel

psychic

biscuit

autumn

mortgage

rhythm

Listen to the sounds

If you can find somebody to record the 44 sounds of English on tape or on CD, and provide you with a written list of them in the right order, then you may find that useful. It can be helpful to have the recording made so that there is a gap after each sound. You could then try copying it. The sound should be repeated on the tape again so that you can check that what you have said sounds exactly right.

Please don't despair if phonics is something you just can't get to grips with. There are many other ways of improving your spelling and it is OK not to be able to 'do phonics'!

So, spelling a word how it sounds isn't always the answer today – but it's interesting to imagine what it would be like! It could be something like this:

*Wee cud hav a lot ov fun deesiding how the wirds wood be spelt. Thair cud eevn bee a computishun to fynd the best nyou werds. I wunder wot the priziz wood bee? Lots ov munny? The charns to reerite the dickshunary? Or just the plezsure of not having to wurry ova how to spell propalee ...

Activity

You might like to try spotting all the words in the last paragraph that have been changed from their usual spellings. The corrected paragraph is at the back of the book.

Things you should know about spelling

Spelling rules

As you have now seen, you don't have to know the spelling rules in order to learn spellings. The difficulty with rules is that you have to remember:

> a. The rule itself
>
> b. Which words to use with the rule
>
> c. The words that don't follow the rule

Here is a typical rule:

> Double the final consonant in a word with a short vowel sound and one syllable, where there is a /f/, /s/, /l/ or /z/ sound at the end.

This works with:

cuff

loss

full

buzz

But the rule doesn't apply to: **yes, as, is, his, has, this, bus, if**.

Some people, however, really enjoy learning the rules and finding out how to use them. There is nothing to stop you learning the rules, as well as the methods shown in this book. There are lots of books which will help you to do this. You will need time, but you may find that you can learn the rules and their exceptions, and are able to apply them on a daily basis.

You have, without knowing it, already learned some rules. A lot of the information on prefixes and suffixes are rules. You have also learned some rules when you looked at syllables. They are very useful and are the rules you can trust the most. Just remember, though, that if you are someone who panics when you are put on the spot and asked to write something in front of someone else, then your knowledge of any traditional spelling rules you have learned might let you down.

Dictionaries and spelling aids

Dictionaries provide us with meanings of words and their spellings. There are many different dictionaries: pocket size, concise, shorter, longer, paperback, hardback– some more helpful than others.

Choosing a dictionary

If you don't yet have a dictionary, take time choosing one and ask yourself these questions:

a. Where will I keep it? A small one can fit into a pocket but won't have as many words as a larger one. You could always decide to have a small one to carry around and a larger one to leave at home.

b. Is the print large enough? If the print is too small to read comfortably then it will put you off using a dictionary. Even if you have good eyesight you are much more likely to use a dictionary if you can read it easily without having to peer at the print.

c. Do the words stand out? Some dictionaries, for example *Chambers Adult Learners' Dictionary*, use colour to make it easy to see the words you are searching for.

d. Do I need a work-related dictionary? Some dictionaries contain just medical or business words.

Go to a good bookshop and look through the dictionaries there before making a decision. It's never a good idea to buy one without seeing it first.

Bigger dictionaries will also give you the following information:

1. How to pronounce a word.

Saying some of the longer words can be difficult. If you have the time to study the pronunciation guide at the front or back of the dictionary, it will help you work out how to pronounce an unfamiliar word.

2. Where a word has come from.

Things you should know about spelling

Some people find that knowing how a word has come into use is interesting. It can make a word easier to remember and that extra knowledge will help to cement the spelling.

3. Other words in the same family.

Finding other words in the same family can be very useful, as you have already discovered. Words such as 'sign' and 'signal' sound different but you can hear the 'sig' in '**sig**nal' and this helps with the spelling of '**sig**n'. Use the dictionary to discover other family members.

4. Spellings of words when suffixes are added.

As already mentioned, adding a suffix can sometimes change the spelling of the base word. A good, big dictionary will give you all the spellings that relate to the base word. If they haven't got room for all of that, they will leave out the easy ones where the suffix is just added on. So don't worry if you can't find the base word plus the suffix. It will probably be just because it is a simple add-on.

Using a dictionary is not straightforward, though, if you are not sure of the first two or three letters of the word you want to look up. For example, the word 'psychology' sounds as though it starts with 's' not 'p', but if you look under letter 's' in the dictionary you will not find the spelling you need. However, there are some spelling dictionaries in which the words are organized by sound. If you look up under the sound /s/ in one of these dictionaries, you will find the correct spelling of 'psychology'.

Electronic dictionaries

There are many small, electronic dictionaries that weigh very little and can be carried around. You can find them in shops or on websites. They are usually referred to as 'spellcheckers'. Some contain dictionary definitions and some will also act as a thesaurus. (A thesaurus is what you use when you want to find other words which mean the same as the one you're looking up. For instance, we often need to use the word 'nice' but don't want to keep repeating ourselves. A thesaurus will give you many other choices such as 'pleasant', 'attractive' or 'delightful'.)

Some of these spellcheckers have a speech facility which means that you can listen to the information. Some will help you with grammar and some with phonics. Prices vary, but generally the more you spend, the more features you will get. They are tiny and fit easily into a pocket. For a small outlay you can buy some 'confidence' knowing that you will still be able to check a spelling even if your dictionary is at home.

Word grids

Wordbar® is a software package that displays a table of words and phrases that sits under the screen where you are typing. It allows you to insert words you need by just clicking on the grid. Specialized grids are available and you can also create your own. For instance, if you run your own business from home and often use the same specialized words then you can make your own grid from those words and always have them handy.

Spellcheckers on computers

Some people find these very useful but others don't. The big problem is that computers don't know when we have used the right word. We might want to type 'their' but we type 'there' instead. The computer will not see that as a mistake because it is a correct spelling. It wouldn't matter so much if there were only a few of these pairs of words but there are about 50 common ones and over 600 altogether, as you have seen in the section on homophones.

This poem shows all the mistakes that a computer will think are OK:

> I have a spelling chequer.
> It came with my PC.
> It plane lee marks four my revue
> Miss steaks aye can knot sea.
> Eye ran this poem threw it,
> I'm shore your pleased two no.
> Its vary polished inn it's weigh.
> My chequer tolled me sew.

It should be written like this:

> I have a spelling **checker**,
> It came with my PC.
> It **plainly** marks **for** my **review**
> **Mistakes I cannot see.**
> I ran this poem **through** it,
> I'm **sure you're** pleased **to know**.
> **It's very** polished **in its way**.
> My **checker told** me **so**.

Keeping any type of dictionary with you is not 'cheating'. In fact it is a tool that everyone should have nearby. No-one can spell every word there is and even very good spellers are used to having access to some sort of dictionary.

Survival skills

An improvement in your spelling will take some time. The strategies described in the first part of this book rely on daily practice and will result in a gradual but very obvious progress over a few weeks. Meanwhile, you will still be faced with the same old difficulties. This section will give you some ideas about what you can do at the same time as you are following the daily routine, and which will make a difference immediately.

Things to say

You may be reading this now because you have found yourself, too many times, in a situation where you feel embarrassed about your spelling. It might have been in the bank, where you've been asked to fill in a form. You might have wanted to join a club but not been able to go through with it because you were worried about having to spell difficult words in front of somebody, on an application form. Perhaps you have been held back at work as your written work doesn't reflect your practical skills.

What do you do in these situations? Do you panic, ask your partner to help or do you just avoid it altogether?

Have you ever thought about what would happen if you said something like:

'Spelling isn't my strong point – would you mind giving me a hand?'

Or 'My spelling isn't always accurate – I hope that won't matter.'

If you are on the telephone you could say:

'Could you spell that please – I'm not sure that I heard you correctly.'

Or 'Could you spell that please – I'd like to make sure I get it right.'

What would happen? Imagine the best and the worst responses. If you know the person, you may be able to gauge the reply. If you don't, you could be risking further embarrassment **but** it might be worth considering a change in how you deal with the situation. Perhaps you could try it out at a time when you know you will be dealing with a sympathetic person.

Things you should know about spelling

We aren't always accurate when we imagine what someone is thinking about us. Would you change your opinion of someone if, for instance, they mentioned that they found maths hard?

Unfortunately, there is no guarantee that by being open about it you are suddenly going to feel better. It will depend entirely upon the reaction of the person you tell. In a work situation it could be something that you would not even consider as you might feel at a disadvantage. All I am suggesting, however, is that you consider that there may be a different way to deal with the situation. In my experience, those people who have treated their spelling difficulties as just one of those things, rather than something to be ashamed of, have felt far less stressed or embarrassed about it. Everyone is different, of course, and you will have to think carefully about whether you can break the habit but do, at least, give it a thought.

Crib sheets

Think about the situations where you find yourself on the spot and getting into a muddle because you can't spell a word. Perhaps you are at work and you often have to write down messages while you are on the phone. Do you find yourself coming across the same words over and over again? If so, start making a list of them – check in a dictionary or other reference book that you have the correct spelling. Then create a small card with those words on in alphabetical order and keep it by the phone. You may need a different crib sheet for different places. If you don't feel confident enough to leave it lying out, then tuck it in a drawer or in the back of a book where you can find it quickly.

Don't despair if you find yourself having to look on the crib sheet for the same word time and time again. Just add it to your weekly list, find the right strategy for it and practise it every day!

Personal dictionary

You may find it easier to carry around with you a small, personalized dictionary. Find one of those very small address books that have the alphabet down the side of the pages. Every time you come across a word that you struggle with, add it to your dictionary (checking that you have found the right spelling first) on the appropriate page. You will be amazed at how much confidence it gives you and you may find yourself remembering the spelling anyway because the element of anxiety and panic has been taken away.

Mobile phone spelling

Most people today carry a mobile phone with them and many of them use predictive text. This is a facility which means that you only have to key in the first two or three letters of a word (if you know them) and it will finish it off for you. This won't work with all phones, or even all words, but it is worth considering. It could act like an electronic spelling dictionary if you find it easy to use. Some phones will store certain words if it has a 'spell' function. It can even help you to learn words. Someone told me that they had learned how to spell the word 'today' by using the predictive text function on their mobile!

Technology

A useful electronic gadget is the Dictaphone®. This is a small voice recorder which could be used in a situation where you would otherwise have to write down what you want to say. Obviously there are certain situations where this would not be practical but equally there are many opportunities in everyday life when the Dictaphone® can be used instead of pen and paper. Then, you take it home, plug it into your PC and what you have said a few hours ago will magically appear on the screen, with everything spelt correctly.

Voice recognition software has been around for a few years now. Recently it has been improved to such an extent that it is very accurate and is far more efficient than the early versions. For people who find spelling a daily struggle, using this software can be a life-changing experience. After an initial, short training session the computer learns to recognize your voice. You can then dictate anything you want to say in word processing, e-mail or other programs.

Proofreading

No matter what you write it is important that you check it in order to make sure that it says exactly what you want to say. Nobody enjoys proofreading their own work, especially if it has been hard enough to produce in the first place. When you have finished, you usually just want to forget about it. However, if you then look carefully through what you have written, you will probably find at least a couple of errors that you hadn't noticed as you were writing.

Writing or word processing can be taxing because when you write you are doing two things at once. Firstly, you are conveying information to the reader. Secondly, you have to convey that information by using a set of conventions to do with punctuation, spelling and grammar. Doing both things at once is not easy because there is so much to remember. You can improve your accuracy by producing a rough draft first, then proofreading it thoroughly before completing a final version which will include any corrections.

Nowadays a lot of people use a computer and a keyboard, as well as pen and paper. There is some help available when using the computer as there is a spellchecker in it. A spelling mistake, as perceived by the computer, will result in a red line underneath the offending word. Even so, you will still have to check everything you have written because homophones (words that sound the same) are not usually indicated as mistakes. If you find it very difficult to distinguish between certain homophones then some software packages will help you to do this.

Unless you are very sure of what you are writing, or you are only leaving a note telling someone that the dinner is in the oven, a thorough check will be needed. When you look back over your work you will not always notice all the mistakes but there is a good chance that you will spot some of them. Check through what you have written but only look for one particular thing at a time. Read it through firstly to check that it makes sense. Read it through again to check for spelling mistakes and read it through a third time to check the punctuation. Each time you re-read you can focus on just the one aspect and you will find it easier to see the mistakes.

Look out for the spelling mistakes that you make over and over again. These are words that you can now learn by finding a way to break them up using 'Look, say, cover, write, check'. Do you notice any patterns? Are you always leaving 'ed' off the ends of words? Do you use the letter 'e' when you should use an 'a'? Do you put 'b' when you mean 'd'? Being aware of the mistakes you usually make will help to prevent you from doing the same thing in the future. It is also a good idea to leave what you have written for a while and do the proofreading when you come back to it later. The spelling mistakes will often seem more obvious once you have had a break from looking at it.

Don't forget that even good spellers need to do a rough draft first.

Here are some points to remember when proofreading for spellings:

- Look at each word closely. It is very easy to miss out a letter. Count the number of letters there are because you will often know how many there in a word, even if you can't remember exactly which letters they are. Checking the number of letters will prompt your memory.

- Try checking your spellings by starting at the end of what you have written and working back to the beginning. Doing this means that you won't be distracted by the sense of what you are saying. You will be able to focus only on the spellings.

- Keep a lookout for homophones. If you regularly make a mistake with, for example, 'to' and 'too', then make it a priority to check those particular words carefully.

- Always look for the mistakes that you know you make, such as missing 'ed' or 's' from the ends of words.

- Ask someone else to check your work for you if you can. A fresh pair of eyes will see the mistakes that you won't.

Things you should know about spelling

Don't be afraid to use the words you want to use, rather than avoiding them because you can't spell them. Add the difficult ones to your list of words to learn and look forward to the pleasure of being able to spell the words you want to use.

Dyslexia

People with dyslexia often find that spelling is a big worry. It stops them writing freely, it can make them feel stupid and it can have a huge impact on their job prospects and social life.

We receive information about words through our ears and our eyes. A dyslexic person's brain will process that information but the messages about the word won't always get through accurately and, when a spelling is produced:

It can have bits missing	*Febuay	(February)
It can be jumbled up	*Apirl	(April)
Or it can have extra chunks	*Octotober	(October)

The methods in this book were designed originally with dyslexic people in mind but, it is a well-known fact that, if you get it right for dyslexics, you get it right for everyone else. So, the methods should suit everyone, whether dyslexic or not.

Symptoms of dyslexia

Poor spelling is not necessarily a sign that someone is dyslexic – it can also be a sign of poor teaching or lack of appropriate schooling. However, if you find it hard to remember the letters or sounds in a word, even when you have been trying to do so for years, it might be because you are dyslexic. You might also find it hard to tell left from right, be unable to use a map or have difficulties with reading. On the plus side, you might be very good with your hands, artistic or very creative. Not everyone with dyslexia has exactly the same symptoms.

Other symptoms include:

- always having struggled with reading and writing, and/or maths at school
- difficulties with short-term memory
- being disorganized

- finding it hard to remember verbal instructions
- difficulties with remembering sequences, such as the alphabet and times tables

Another common symptom is experiencing what is known as visual stress when looking at text on a white page. The words can seem blurred or even appear to move. For more on visual stress see the following section.

All of the above symptoms can be mild, severe or anything in between. Some of them do not become obvious until a higher academic level is reached. For instance, someone might cope very well with GCSEs and A-levels but, with the increased demands of a degree course, suddenly find that they are unexpectedly struggling. Similarly, many adults get by at school but then find that they can't cope in the workplace.

Adults who suffer with literacy problems because of their dyslexia are often not aware that along with the difficulties can also come benefits. Many dyslexics are very good with their hands. They are often excellent at DIY and will rarely need instructions, measurements or plans. They are able to see what they want to make in their mind's eye, in all three dimensions, and only need a quick glance at something before going off to create it. An art college will usually contain about twice the national average of dyslexics, and many dyslexics will naturally gravitate towards such professions as hairdressing, building, architecture, engineering and graphic design.

Causes of dyslexia

Over recent years there has been much research into what causes dyslexia. There is, as yet, no overall agreement and the discussions and research are continuing in many parts of the country and overseas. Some scientists think that there is a difficulty in interpreting the messages that are received through the eyes or ears. Others feel that there is a problem with storing the sounds when they are first heard as a child. There is also the theory that a part of the brain does not function as it should. Some researchers think that all three of these situations occur at the same time and combine together to cause the difficulties that dyslexic people commonly face.

It is also fairly common to find that dyslexia runs in families. It has been shown that there is a strong genetic link, and chromosomes have been identified which carry the 'dyslexia gene'.

All of the research is being used to identify the most effective support that can be given to dyslexic children and adults. Most people agree, however, that there is no cure for dyslexia. However, some dyslexic people, when asked, would rather have their dyslexia than not. They have realized what the benefits are and are happy to accept their poor spelling or reading because they enjoy the positive side of the condition. Many have good lateral thinking skills, or the ability to see the whole picture. Lots of dyslexic adults that I have worked with have an ability to think in pictures and this stands them in good stead in whatever career path they have chosen. Many famous dyslexic people, such as Leonardo da Vinci, Agatha Christie, Albert Einstein and Roald Dahl might not have achieved all they did without the advantages of dyslexia.

One person, however, does believe that dyslexia can be cured. Wynford Dore founded a programme which involves following a daily exercise routine for one year on average. He argues that these exercises will alter a part of the brain and improve many problems associated with dyslexia. He has seen many success stories and I have worked with a student who completed the programme. Now she doesn't need my help any more. Details of his book can be found at the back, but be aware that the programme is expensive and not everyone is accepted on it.

Why can dyslexia be a problem?

Before a standardized spelling system was accepted in this country, dyslexia was not seen to be a problem. Variations in spelling were the norm and nobody minded when a word was spelt in different ways as long as it could be understood. Shakespeare regularly spelt the same word in different ways. There is even evidence that shows that he signed his own name differently on separate occasions. With the advent of the printing press came a far less relaxed regime. It was also the privilege of richer people to have been educated, so it wasn't long before society viewed people who were literate as people who were well educated and, therefore, well thought of. Well-educated people knew the correct writing conventions, would have excellent handwriting and would, of course, know how to spell.

Most of us want to appear well educated because it gives us a higher social standing and it allows us to feel better about ourselves. Self-esteem and self-confidence, both of which stem from feeling good about ourselves, are two of the strongest foundations for happiness. Many dyslexic adults have low self-esteem and very little self-confidence because they were made to feel bad about themselves when growing up. Now that there is a greater awareness of dyslexia let's hope that this will happen less and less. However, it may take many years before the perceived stigma of being a poor speller will be eradicated.

What to do if you think you are dyslexic

1. Do not feel alone! Between 4% and 10% of the population are thought to have dyslexia. It is known as a hidden disability so you won't know if the person sitting beside you on the bus struggles in the same way that you do, or whether the person behind you in the queue at the bank is as nervous as you are about having to fill in a form.

2. Find out more about it. Understand that it's not your fault – it has a physical basis. There are many books and websites which will give you a lot more information. See the suggestions at the end of this book.

3. Undergo a screening for dyslexia. There is a short, easy screening checklist included at the end of the book. Based on the result and your own feelings, you could then have an assessment to find out whether or not you are dyslexic.

4. Don't despair as there is a lot of help available.

   a. If you are a **student at university or college** – go along to your support department. There, you should be offered an assessment of your needs and all the help that will enable you to complete your course. This could be anything from study skills support to training on software packages which have been designed with dyslexics in mind.

b. If you are on a **training course** – your training provider is obliged to offer you all the help and support you need to obtain your qualification.

c. If you are **unemployed** – you could attend literacy or numeracy classes at a college of further education.

d. If you are **in employment** – your employer is legally bound to ensure that you are able to carry out your job by making what is known as *reasonable adjustments* to help you. Funding could be available through government agencies – ask about this at your local job centre. You will have to decide whether you want to be open about your difficulties. You could also attend literacy or numeracy classes at college in the evening.

However, it is important to remember that dyslexia is a collection of many symptoms and the fact that you struggle with spelling doesn't necessarily mean that you are dyslexic.

Visual stress

Visual stress, sometimes known as scotopic sensitivity or Meares-Irlen Syndrome, is a condition which can be suffered by dyslexics and non-dyslexics alike. It is not a condition which the general public knows much about but it can be very debilitating for people who suffer with it. Many people struggle for years without understanding that it is not normal and can easily be corrected.

Sufferers can experience the blurring or apparent movement of text on white paper and, in some extreme cases, letters appear to drop off the page. Individual letters can merge into one another and be very difficult to identify. They can also appear incomplete, as though they are formed of dashes rather than continual straight lines. Bright, white paper will glare and appear to overpower the words.

People with this condition often find it very uncomfortable to sit under fluorescent lighting for any length of time. They find it difficult to read from a whiteboard, particularly if the light is shining on it. A glaring computer screen will also be uncomfortable or cause headaches, as will the lights from oncoming car headlights at night.

You can imagine that reading will be hard if a person suffers from visual stress. It is also the case that spelling can prove to be difficult as well. Proficient readers read by rapid visual recognition of two or three words at once. They see the word's shape and general appearance, and match it very quickly with what is stored in their visual memory. If, over the years, they have been unable to store a clear picture of a word, then the spelling will not be easy to recall when they need to write it.

If you feel that any of the above applies to you then try looking at some text on a white page with a plastic coloured sheet over it. You may have a plastic folder or ring-binder which has coloured, transparent front and back covers. If the words appear to be clearer through the coloured layer then you may benefit from using a coloured overlay when you read. If you see no difference at all then you probably don't have the syndrome. (Several companies supply packs of coloured overlays. See the suggested sources at the back of the book.)

If you want to investigate this further then it would be helpful to be assessed by an optician who has an Intuitive Colorimeter. Not every optician has this particular piece of equipment so it will be worth finding one who has. They should be able to give you an indication of whether coloured overlays will help you or whether you need to use coloured lenses in a pair of glasses. It is important to remember that visual stress has nothing to do with how good or bad your eyesight is. It is a good idea to have a full eyesight test when being assessed as this can sometimes reveal other previously undiagnosed visual problems.

Things you should know about spelling

The history of spelling

People often ask, 'Why aren't words just spelt as they sound?'
Interestingly, there was a time when they were. Over the years, however,
our spoken language has altered but our spellings haven't changed to
reflect how words sound now.

The English language is a modern, living language but also one that
reflects a fascinating history. Each time Britain was invaded, so too was
the language and, in the words we use now, we have been left with
reminders of the different nations who conquered British shores.

It is because we have had so many influences on our language in
the past that we have so many apparently strange spellings. An
understanding of how words have developed can make learning these
spellings more interesting and less frustrating. Knowing where our words
have come from can help you to feel better about those infuriating groups
of letters that seem to make no sense at all.

Influences on English spelling

For many hundreds of years our language was only a spoken language.
There was never much need to write anything down until people stopped
travelling around and decided to settle in one place. Then it was decided
that it would be useful to make records of who owned which bit of land
and what had been bought or sold.

The English language truly originated a great distance away from
England and our alphabet stems from one that was created around
1000 BC by the Ancient Greeks. The first writing system discovered in
Britain is one that consisted of sets of straight lines. This was followed
by a system known as 'runes' which looks more like the letters we are
familiar with today. Here are some examples:

The Anglo-Saxon people who came to the British Isles from Germany and settlers from Scandinavia all introduced their own words to the language. Many of these words are completely unrecognisable today but some you would still be able to understand, such as cwic (quick) and cwene (queen).

By 1066 Britain had language with standardized spellings known as Old English, or Anglo-Saxon. However, this was the year that England was invaded by the Normans and the course of the English language changed dramatically. Duke William of Normandy came over from France and, after winning the Battle of Hastings, was crowned King of England. He and his courtiers brought the French language with them and, because they replaced many English aristocrats, the language of the upper classes became French. The working classes, however, kept the Anglo-Saxon English and, for a while, the country had two languages.

In time, the two languages merged and by around 1400 words were spelt as they were pronounced, with some variations in the spellings depending upon where people lived and their local accents and dialects.

The next big event in the history of our language was the development of the printing press. In 1476 William Caxton introduced the printing press to England, and so led the movement to ensure that there was only one acceptable spelling for each word. In order to produce a standard set of words he needed to decide which group of spellings would best suit his purpose. Although he was sometimes uncertain, he favoured the pronunciations and spellings from the East Midlands and London area. It made sense to bring some sort of regularity to the language now that it was to be captured in print. Even the printing process in itself, though, played a part in some of the spellings we have today. Extra letters would be added to words, or sometimes taken off, when printers needed to fit a certain number of words on to a line. Some of the printers were Dutch and would insert Dutch spellings into English words. A classic example of this is the word 'yacht'. It was 'yott' before it was altered. Those amended spellings were eventually accepted as standard and we are left to struggle with them today.

Things you should know about spelling

The changes that were made

We can trace the origins of many of these spelling decisions. Look at the examples of 'hope' and 'Pete'. In 1582 the scholar Richard Mulcaster decreed that by putting an 'e' on to the ends of words, it would make the earlier vowel change its sound. So, without the second 'e' 'Pete' would be 'pet' and 'hope' would be 'hop'. This has proved a very popular rule and we use it a lot today, sometimes referring to it as the 'magic e' or 'silent e'. Unfortunately, we still have some words that end with 'e' when the vowel **doesn't** change its sound – 'some' and 'have' being good examples. (This is a good illustration of why learning the rules isn't always helpful.)

Many of our irregular words used to be pronounced as they are spelt. For instance, some words that begin with 'wh' used to begin with 'hw' and both letters were pronounced as separate sounds. Apparently the change was made so that they would match the 'ch' and 'th' words that we already had.

The silent 'k' at the beginning of words such as 'knee' and 'knock' was not always silent. Over the years the pronunciation has changed but the spelling has remained the same. You can 'say it oddly' to help you remember the spelling by pronouncing it as it used to be said.

How word origin can help you

The spelling of the word 'holiday' can cause problems. It will often appear as *hoilday. This can be because:

- 'oi' is more common than 'io'
- the letter 'i' looks like the letter 'l' so can be mistaken visually
- the middle of a word is often the hardest bit to remember accurately
- SID is forgotten and the separate syllabes – hol/id/ay – are not heard slowly and on their own

Knowing where the word comes from might help to overcome the problem. It is from two words – 'holy' and 'day' and people would have the day off on a Holy Day. So you can see how, over time, the word has become 'holiday' and means 'time off work' or 'a period of time spent away from home, for recreation'. When you want to spell the word, remember the word 'holy' and that you only have to change the 'y' to an 'i'.

Saturday comes from 'Saturn's day' so if you can spell the name of the planet Saturn, remembering the 'u', it will help you with 'Saturday'.

Some dictionaries, the larger ones in particular, will tell you about the origins of words as well as their meanings. This example from *The Chambers Dictionary* gives us the information that the word 'alphabet' comes from two words, 'alpha' and 'beta'. These two words are the names of the first two letters of the Greek alphabet.

Gr *alphabetos*, from *alpha* and *beta*, the first two Greek letters

There are also etymological dictionaries which go into a word's development in more depth. (Etymology is an account of the origins and the developments in the meaning of a word.) The explanation of a word's origins will often be difficult to understand as it is usually abbreviated and will look quite complicated. However, if you are interested in finding out about where a particular word has come from then it is worth persevering. The abbreviations will be explained either at the beginning or at the back of the dictionary and, once you are familiar with them, will be easier to use.

The future of spelling

The English language is constantly changing as we invent new words. There are so many words invented that in order to be included in *The Chambers Dictionary* a new word must have been used in a variety of places, over a period of a few years. The dictionary includes some older words that are now no longer in use, but most dictionaries have been edited to include only words that are in use now.

Over the years there have been many calls for spelling to be made more 'transparent' or for words to be spelt as they sound. Our language is based on an alphabet where the letters are designed to represent sounds. As we have seen, our spoken language has changed a lot over the last 1000 years but, unlike some other countries, we have not brought our spellings up to date. The Simplified Spelling Society was formed in 1908 with an aim to update English spelling. They believe that simplified spellings would save teachers time at school, as well as making spellings easier to learn for people whose first language is not English. As yet they have met with little success but still produce newsletters, leaflets and books which aim to promote spelling reform. However, it is unlikely that there will be any such changes as it would involve major upheavals in countless organizations and, of course, a substantial cost. There is also a lack of agreement as to which system should be used and there are doubts that an old and a new system could work together, which they would have to for a number of years.

So what will happen in the future? Will texting language and spelling take over? Will 'C U L8R' and '2moro' ever be accepted as correct anywhere other than on a mobile phone? Well, we have been texting for a few years now and there has been no significant alteration of normal spellings. Many people use predictive text which saves time and will spell words for you, so perhaps this is why we are not inundated with peculiar spellings yet.

We also see strange looking words which have been created by companies which employ an increasingly flexible artistic licence. We see 'lite' (instead of light) on yoghurt pots and 'and' abbreviated to 'n' as in 'fish 'n' chips'. 'Right' is often spelt 'rite', and you will often see signs such as 'Xpress Dry Cleaning While U Wait'.

As technology advances we will see the invention of many more words. It seems strange that there was a time when words such as 'cyberspace' and 'website' didn't exist. Who knows what new words will enter our language in the future? What will be certain though, is that some will be harder to spell than others!

ANSWERS
TO ACTIVITIES

Small words (page 23)

1. Monday – on, day
2. computer – put, compute
3. really – all, ally, real
4. comfort – or, for, fort
5. football – all, ball, foot
6. amateur – am, at, ate, mat, mate
7. tragedy – rag, age, aged, rage, raged
8. choreography – or, ore, rap, graph, chore, choreograph
9. interesting – in, tin, rest, inter, sting, resting, interest
10. knowledgeable – no, ow, now, owl, led, edge, able, know, ledge, knowledge

Prefixes and suffixes (page 32)

1. (un)employ(ment)
2. (im)polite(ly)
3. (dis)member(ed)
4. (inter)nation(al)
5. (mis)(under)stand(ing)
6. writing   write
7. happiness   happy
8. stopping   stop
9. maker   make
10. coping   cope
11. (un)pleasant
12. (tri)angle
13. (sub)marine
14. (trans)action
15. (dis)appear

Say it oddly (page 37)

1.	knot	k not
2.	orchestra	or chest ra
3.	massacre	mass acre
4.	crystal	cry stal
5.	usual	us u – as in 'you' Al
6.	special	spec – as in speck i – as in 'eye' Al
7.	parliament	par lia – as in the girl's name ment
8.	radiator	radi a tor
9.	Thames	say Thames to rhyme with 'names' – pronounce the first two letters as you would at the start of 'then'
10.	opinion	o pini on

Syllables (page 43)

1.	slo/gan	Open syllable
2.	trum/pet	Closed syllable
3.	join/ing	Two vowels together make one sound
4.	sub/urb	Vowel sound made by a vowel and a consonant
5.	com/plete	Syllable with 'e' at the end but not pronounced
6.	op/tion	Common syllable – this one is a suffix

Memory tricks (page 49)

1. Draw a picture to help you remember the spelling of 'parallel'.

You could have drawn a picture showing two horizontal parallel lines in the middle of the word:

para=el

2. Make up a saying using all, or some of, the letters of 'Britain'.

You could say that a 'Brit always interprets noisily'.

3. Fill in the missing word to complete this sentence: An island is land.

4. Make up a sentence using some of the following words: lamb, comb, numb, thumb, crumb, tomb.

There are many possibilities, but how about: 'Combing the lamb made my thumb numb.'

Word families (page 64)

Here are some suggestions:

1. fu**ture**, punc**ture** and crea**ture**

2. l**air**, ch**air**s and rep**air**

3. br**ake**, t**ake** and f**ake**

4. rej**oi**ce, v**oi**ce and disapp**oi**ntment

5. **str**etch, **str**ing and **str**ess

Test yourself (page 64)

1. college – *Small words*   As the difficulty tends to be with the first 'e', it would be a good idea to home in on that area. The other two letters around it make the word '**leg**'. Now you need to link that word **leg** with college. Perhaps you could come up with a sentence like 'Col**leg**e will give you a **leg** up with your qualifications'.

2. culminate – *Syllables*   I would be tempted to split this word into syllables. It has three, each with three letters – 'cul' 'min' and 'ate'.

3. rhyme – *Memory trick*   One way to deal with this is to use a memory trick. If you can remember the sentence '**r**hyme **h**as **y**our **m**ind **e**ntertained', you will remember the spelling. The first letter of each word in the sentence spells the word.

4. virtual – *Say it oddly*   You could say 'vir' 'tu' 'al'.

5. medicine – *Word families*   Luckily we have two very helpful words which belong with medicine – medi**c** and medi**c**al. Both of those tell you that the letter 's' is not in medi**c**ine because you can hear the /c/ sound.

6. kitchen – *Say it oddly/Memory trick*   Say the word '**kit**' and you will remember the letter 't'. You could think of someone's football **kit** all over the **kit**chen floor – waiting to be washed!

7. gross – *Memory trick*   If you know someone called Ross who is gross, then you're in luck. If you don't, then you could imagine someone to fit that description!

8. unfortunately – *Prefixes and suffixes*   As soon as you take off the prefix and two suffixes this word becomes much simpler. The base word is 'fortune'. To make it into 'fortunate' you must drop the 'e' at the end of 'fortune'. To make it into 'fortunately', you just add 'ly'. The prefix attaches to the beginning of the word. Look back at the few rules you learned for adding suffixes. Do you remember that when you add a suffix that starts with a vowel to a word that ends with an 'e', you have to drop the 'e'?

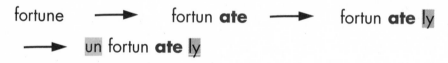

fortune ⟶ fortun **ate** ⟶ fortun **ate** ly

⟶ un fortun **ate** ly

9. season – *Small words/Memory trick*   How about this sentence: This is the season to be on the high seas.

10. effectiveness – *Prefixes and suffixes*   The base word is 'effect'. Then two suffixes have been added: 'ive' and 'ness'. There are no changes of spelling because 'effect' ends with a consonant.

11. through – *Word families*   The best way to remember this difficult group of words is to link them in pairs. For instance, you could say, 'He hit the golf ball th**rough** the **rough**'. This works as long as you can spell the word 'rough'. (You might like to remember this sentence as well: 'She th**ought** that she **ought** to go for a walk.')

12. anecdotal – *Syllables*   This word splits into syllables that you should be able to hear if you slow it down: an / ec / do / tal.

Homophones (page 84)

1. The **two** boys were asked if they wanted **to** come to the football match **too**.

2. **They're** off on **their** holidays tomorrow and will be travelling **there** by car.

3. **It's** nearly Autumn and time for the tree to shed **its** leaves.

4. They will decide **whether** they go or not when they see what the **weather** is like.

5. There was more than one **witch** at the Hallowe'en party but it was difficult to say **which** one had the best costume.

6. The picture had been painted **by** a famous artist but the man did not have enough money to **buy** it.

7. She had just bought a new dress but didn't know **where** she would be able to **wear** it.

8. After his football **practice** he decided to **practise** riding downhill on his skateboard.

9. The woman from the council has given permission to **license** the new wine bar and will send the owners an alcohol **licence** later in the week.

Phonics – silent letters (page 104)

lam**b**	'b' is silent
We**d**nesday	'd' is silent
kneel	'k' is silent
psychic	'p' is silent
bisc**u**it	'u' is silent
autum**n**	'n' is silent
mor**t**gage	't' is silent
r**h**ythm	'h' is silent

Phonics – last paragraph (page 105)

This is the paragraph with the words correctly spelt:

> We could have a lot of fun deciding how the words would be spelt. There could even be a competition to find the best new words. I wonder what the prizes would be? Lots of money? The chance to rewrite the dictionary? Or just the pleasure of not having to worry over how to spell properly ...

List of difficult words

The following words are often spelt wrongly. You could try learning some of these during the four weeks:

absence, accept, accidentally, accommodate, achieved, acknowledge, acquainted, addresses, aerial, agreeable, amateur, among, anxiety, appearance, appropriate, argument, arrangements, athletic, Autumn, awful

beginning, believed, benefited, breathe, Britain, business

calendar, captain, ceiling, cemetery, certain, choice, clothes, college, coming, commitment, committee, completely, conscientious, conscious, consistent, convenience, copies, course, courteous, courtesy, criticism

deceive, decision, definite, desirable, diarrhoea, disappointed, disastrous, discipline, dissatisfied

efficiency, eighth, embarrassed, essential, exaggerated, excellent, exercise, exhausted, existence, expense, experience

familiar, February, financial, foreign, forty, friend

gauge, genius, government, grammar, grievance, guardian

harass, height, heroes, hierarchy, honorary, humorous, hungry, hurriedly, hypocrisy

imagination, immediately, incidentally, independent, indispensable, influential, inoculate, intelligence, irresistible

knowledge, know, knew

library, literature, lose, losing, lying

maintenance, marriage, meant, medicine, Mediterranean, millennium, miniature, minuscule, minutes, mischievous, misspell, murmur

necessary, niece, nothing, noticeable

occasional, occurred, occurrence, omitted, opinion, opportunity, originally

parallel, parliament, passed, pastime, permanent, permissible, perseverance, physical, pleasant, possesses, preceding, preference,

List of difficult words

prejudice, principal, principle, privilege, procedure, proceeds, professional, professor, pronunciation, psychiatry, psychiatrist, psychology, psychologist, publicly

quiet, questionnaire

really, received, recognized (or recognised), recommended, referred, relieved, repetition, restaurant, rhythm

scarcely, science, secretaries, seize, sentence, separate, sergeant, severely, shining, similar, sincerely, speech, stationary, stationery, strength, successful, supersede, surprising, synonym

tedious, tendency, tragedy, transferred, twelfth

unconscious, unnecessary, until, usually

valuable, view

Wednesday, weird, withhold, writing

you're

Glossary

affix   a group of letters which can be added to the beginning or end of a base word. It will change its meaning or create a new word.

apostrophe   a punctuation sign which shows:
1. missing letters where words have been joined together but lost one or more letters – don't = do not
2. ownership by something or someone – the cat's tail (the tail belongs to the cat)

auditory memory   a memory for sounds

base word   a word to which a prefix or suffix can be added to make another word – mean + t = meant

compound word   a word made from two other words – 'snowman'

consonant   letters of the alphabet other than a, e, i, o, u. The letter 'y' can be a consonant as in the word 'yes' or a vowel as in 'happy'.

irregular word   a word that is not spelt as it sounds – 'yacht'

lower case   small letters – letters that are not capitals

motor memory   a memory for movement

neurolinguistic programming	NLP – a system of therapy that studies conscious and unconscious human behaviour. It aims to use this knowledge to 'programme' the brain and improve an aspect of life.
noun	a word that names somebody or something – 'table', 'love'
phoneme	the smallest unit of sound in a word. A phoneme can be represented by one, two, three or four letters – /e/ as in 'egg', /ee/ as in 'feet'.
phonics	a method of teaching reading and spelling that is based on understanding the link between letters and sounds in a word
plural	a word (noun) that means there is more than one of the thing it is naming – 'boats', 'children'
prefix	a group of letters that can be added to the beginning of a word to change its meaning – un + certain = uncertain
regular word	a word that is spelt as it sounds – 'dog', 'plan'
sentence	a group of words that makes sense. A sentence needs a capital letter at the beginning and a full stop at the end. It should have a verb as well.
suffix	a group of letters that can be added to the end of a word to change the way that word is used – 'start' + 'ing' becomes 'starting'. Sometimes the spelling of the base word changes when the suffix is added – 'make' + 'ing' becomes 'making'.

syllable   a letter, or group of letters, within a word and which contains a vowel sound

thesaurus   a book that lists words with the same or similar meaning together

verb   a 'doing' or a 'being' word – 'think', 'read'

visual memory   a memory for what is seen

vowel   the letters a, e, i, o,u. (The letter 'y' can act as a vowel too.) A vowel sound can be made by a vowel on its own, two vowels together or a vowel and a consonant together (for example, 'ay').

Dyslexia screening checklist

The following questions will help you decide if you might be dyslexic.

Answer each question Yes or No. Do not miss any questions out. If you are in any doubt, give whichever feels like the truer answer.

1	When using the telephone, do you get the numbers mixed up when you dial?	YES	NO
2	Is your spelling poor?	YES	NO
3	When you write down the date, do you often make mistakes?	YES	NO
4	Do you mix up dates and times and miss appointments?	YES	NO
5	Do you find forms difficult and confusing?	YES	NO
6	Do you find it difficult to take messages on the phone and pass them on correctly?	YES	NO
7	Do you mix up bus numbers like 35 and 53?	YES	NO
8	Do you find it difficult to say the months of the year forwards in a fluent manner?	YES	NO
9	When you were at school, did you find it hard to learn the multiplication or times tables?	YES	NO
10	Do you take longer than you should to read a page of a book?	YES	NO
11	Do you find difficulty in telling left from right?	YES	NO
12	Did you find it difficult to decide how to answer these questions?	YES	NO

In the line below, count the points given for each YES answer. For example, count 3 points if you answered YES to question 1.

Question number	1	2	3	4	5	6	7	8	9	10	11	12
Points scored for YES	**3**	**3**	**3**	**3**	**3**	**2**	**2**	**2**	**2**	**2**	**2**	**3**

In the line of boxes below, mark one box for each point you scored.

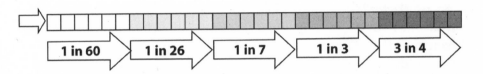

This tells you how likely you are to be dyslexic. 1 in 7 is an above average chance.

Of course, it is always possible for you to be in the 1 in 60 with a low score who is not dyslexic. Your own feelings about the matter can sometimes be more significant than the score.

Useful books and websites

Books about spelling

A Speller's Companion	Margaret E Brown and Hugh L Brown	Brown & Brown
Magical Spelling	Jenny Foster	Available from Inner Sense (email innersense@aol.com)
Tree or Three?: An Elementary Pronunciation Course (includes audio CD)	Ann Baker	Cambridge University Press

Although this last book is designed to help with pronunciation, it will also give you practice in hearing the separate sounds in words.

Writing guide

Chambers Adult Learners' Writing Guide	Ruth Thornton	Chambers Harrap Publishers

Dictionaries

Chambers Adult Learners' Dictionary		Chambers Harrap Publishers
The Ace Spelling Dictionary	David Moseley	LDA

Websites

www.bbc.co.uk/skillswise	covers many aspects of spelling as well as grammar etc
www.spellingsociety.org	the Simplified Spelling Society
www.avantibooks.com	a book supplier with more self-access spelling books for adults

Books on dyslexia

Making Dyslexia Work for You	Vicki Goodwin and Bonita Thomson	David Fulton Publishers
Dyslexia – The Miracle Cure	Wynford Dore	John Blake Publishing Ltd

Websites on dyslexia

www.bdadyslexia.org.uk	British Dyslexia Association
www.adult-dyslexia.org	Adult Dyslexia Organisation
www.dyslexiaaction.org.uk	Dyslexia Action
www.dyslexic.com	specialists in computers and software for those with dyslexia

Coloured overlays – suppliers

Cerium Visual Technologies (www.ceriumvistech.co.uk)

The Dyslexia Shop (www.thedyslexiashop.co.uk)

Crossbow Education (www.crossboweducation.com)

Useful books and websites

Crossbow also supply Reading Rulers which are coloured, rectangular and have thick guide lines printed on them which helps to keep the eye on the right line of text.

Word grids – suppliers

Crick software (www.learninggrids.com)

Index

Index